FROM TRAIL TO RAILWAY

KENNIKAT PRESS SCHOLARLY REPRINTS
Dr. Ralph Adams Brown, Senior Editor

Series on
MAN AND HIS ENVIRONMENT
Under the General Editorial Supervision of
Dr. Roger C. Heppell
Professor of Geography, State University of New York

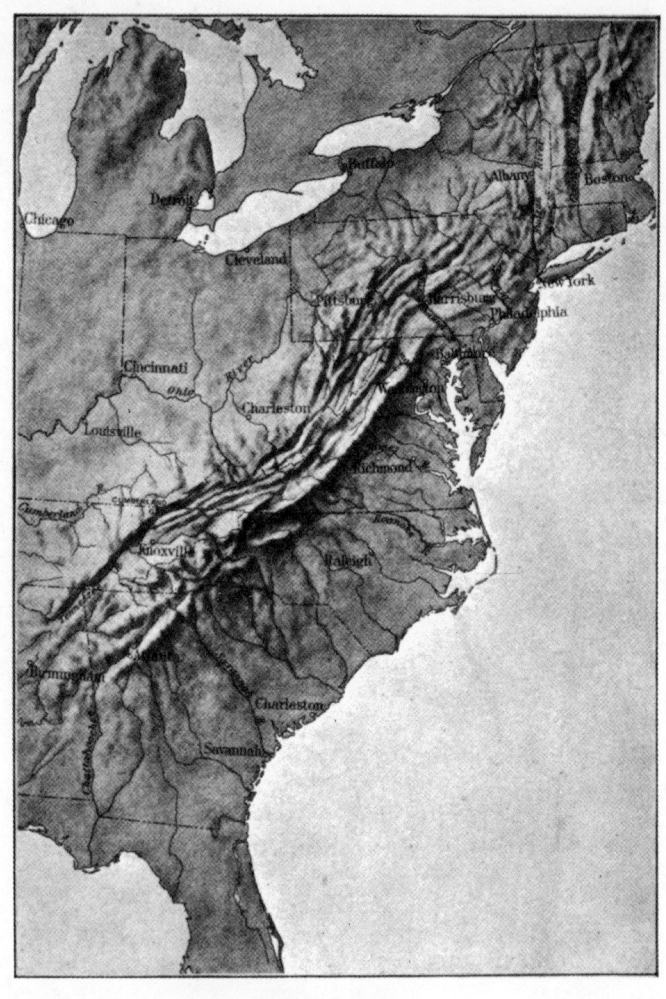

SCALE OF MILES
50 0 50 100 150 200

EASTERN UNITED STATES

FROM TRAIL TO RAILWAY
THROUGH
THE APPALACHIANS

BY

ALBERT PERRY BRIGHAM, A.M.

KENNIKAT PRESS
Port Washington, N. Y./London

FROM TRAIL TO RAILWAY

First published in 1907
Reissued in 1970 by Kennikat Press
Library of Congress Catalog Card No: 78-113279
ISBN 0-8046-1317-6

Manufactured by Taylor Publishing Company   Dallas, Texas

KENNIKAT SERIES ON MAN AND HIS ENVIRONMENT

PREFACE

This book grows out of the conviction that geography in the schools must return somewhat to human interests. In saying this the author will scarcely need to defend himself against the charge of undervaluing physiography. It is only a question of wise adaptation to youthful students. Elementary history also needs to be placed in its setting of physical conditions. It is here attempted to promote both these objects in the study of the eastern United States. If geography and history can be well correlated, both of these great themes may be taught with economy of time and with stronger interest.

Much more might be said concerning the growth of centers, the agriculture, and the commerce, but the limits of space are rigid. Hence roads and westward movements have been made the main topic. The geography is not taught formally, but is woven in with the story. Care has been given to the maps of the several regions, that they should clearly express the essentials and avoid the vagueness of many small-scale representations of the Appalachian belt.

A. P. B.

COLGATE UNIVERSITY
   October, 1906

CONTENTS

Chapter		Page
I.	Boston and the Berkshires	1
II.	Pioneers of the Mohawk and the Hudson	14
III.	Oriskany, a Battle of the Revolution	29
IV.	The Erie Canal	40
V.	The New York Central Railway	53
VI.	Old Journeys from Philadelphia to the West	63
VII.	The Pennsylvania Railroad	74
VIII.	The National Road	86
IX.	The Baltimore and Ohio Railroad	98
X.	Cities of the Ohio Valley	111
XI.	The Great Valley	129
XII.	To Kentucky by the Cumberland Gap	142
XIII.	Frontier Soldiers and Statesmen	155
XIV.	Cities of the Southern Mountains	167
Index		183

LIST OF ILLUSTRATIONS

Figure		Page
1.	Cunard Steamship	3
2.	Union Station, Springfield	6
3.	Deerfield Valley, Charlemont, Mass.	8
4.	Eastern Portal of Hoosac Tunnel	11
5.	South Station, Boston	12
6.	Henry Hudson	16
7.	Sir William Johnson	20
8.	Genesee Street, Utica	23
9.	Old Fort Johnson, Amsterdam, New York	26
10.	Oriskany Battle Monument	30
11.	Herkimer directing the Battle of Oriskany	33
12.	Herkimer's Monument and Mansion	36
13.	De Witt Clinton	43
14.	Erie Canal, Utica	46
15.	Erie Canal, Syracuse	48
16.	Traveling by Packet on the Erie Canal	50
17.	Erie Canal and Solvay Works, Syracuse	51
18.	De Witt Clinton Train	54
19.	Twentieth Century Limited	57
20.	Rounding the Noses, Mohawk Valley	59
21.	Penn Square, Lancaster, Pennsylvania	65
22.	Bridge over Conestoga Creek, Lancaster, Pennsylvania	67
23.	Tollhouse near Lancaster, Pennsylvania	68
24.	Hambright's Hotel, on the "Lancaster Pike"	70
25.	Old Road House, Chambersburg, Pennsylvania	71
26.	Freight Locomotive, Pennsylvania Railroad	75
27.	Tunnel, Portage Railway	76
28.	Broad Street Station, Philadelphia	77
29.	Bridge, Pennsylvania Railroad, above Harrisburg	79
30.	Pennsylvania Railroad Shops, Altoona	80
31.	Horseshoe Curve, Pennsylvania Railroad	81
32.	Rock Cut, Pennsylvania Railroad	84
33.	Tollhouse near Brownsville, Pennsylvania	87
34.	Milestone, Braddock's Road, Frostburg, Maryland	90
35.	Old Road House, Brownsville, Pennsylvania	92
36.	Cumberland and Gap in Wills Mountain	95
37.	Bridge and Monument, National Road, near Wheeling, West Virginia	96
38.	Mount Royal Station, Baltimore	99

LIST OF ILLUSTRATIONS

FIGURE		PAGE
39.	Chesapeake and Ohio Canal, Cumberland	100
40.	Highest Point on Baltimore and Ohio Railroad, Sand Patch, Pennsylvania	103
41.	Down the Potomac from Harpers Ferry	106
42.	Coke Ovens, Meyersdale, Pennsylvania	108
43.	The Observation End, Baltimore and Ohio Railroad	110
44.	Old Blockhouse, Pittsburg	112
45.	Pittsburg	115
46.	Coal Barges, Pittsburg	119
47.	Pittsburg at Night	120
48.	Furnaces near Pittsburg	121
49.	River Front, Cincinnati	125
50.	Luray, Shenandoah Valley	131
51.	James River Gap in the Blue Ridge	134
52.	Hilly Farm Lands, near Knoxville	136
53.	Great Valley, from the Pinnacle, Cumberland Gap	139
54.	Cumberland Gap from the East	143
55.	Daniel Boone	145
56.	Pineville Gap, Cumberland River	147
57.	Cornfield near Cumberland Gap	150
58.	Kentucky Blue Grass	152
59.	Three States Monument, Cumberland Gap	153
60.	George Rogers Clark	157
61.	On the French Broad	159
62.	John Sevier	162
63.	James Robertson	164
64.	Sevier Monument, Knoxville	165
65.	Old Statehouse, Knoxville	166
66.	Street in Knoxville	168
67.	On the Campus, University of Tennessee	169
68.	Marble Quarry near Knoxville	171
69.	Statehouse, Nashville	173
70.	Chattanooga from Cameron Hill	175
71.	Broad Street, Atlanta	177
72.	Fulton Bag and Cotton Mills, Atlanta	178
73.	Georgia Institute of Technology, Atlanta	179
74.	Iron Furnace, Birmingham	180

MAPS

Eastern United States	*Frontispiece*	
New England	Facing page	4
New York	" "	26
Pennsylvania	" "	64
Southern Appalachian Region	" "	132

FROM TRAIL TO RAILWAY

FROM TRAIL TO RAILWAY

CHAPTER I

BOSTON AND THE BERKSHIRES

From the time of the settlement of Massachusetts Boston has had a large share of the business of the country. Her natural advantages are great. On the one hand there is her harbor, sheltered by many islands from the storms of the Atlantic ; on the other are tidal rivers and level highways leading to the interior of the state. Emerson, who was born in Boston, wrote :

> Each street leads downward to the sea,
> Or landward to the west.

For generations, as the city has grown, her people have been crowding back the ocean by filling in the shallows, and now her busy streets extend over acres of "made land," while from the south, the west, and the north, lines of railway connect her with all parts of America.

Not many years after the War of the Revolution a Boston merchant ship went around the world. She took on board a native at Hawaii, sold her load of furs in Canton, rounded Cape Horn, and anchored at length in Boston harbor. So great an achievement did this seem that Governor Hancock and the people said fine things and made merry.

This little ship was eighty-three feet long, and you could measure off seven or eight times her length on one of the big liners of to-day. Later the same ship set sail again, and on the west coast of America, in one of the roughest seas, her master, Captain Gray, saw the mouth of a great river. He was determined to enter it. Having crossed the breakers, he sailed up the river more than twenty miles, and to-day it bears the name of his ship, the *Columbia*. Boston was reaching out into the wide world. Many years later this discovery had much to do with securing the rights of the United States in the Oregon country against the claims of Great Britain.

Young lads often went out on these voyages, and the training made them strong men. There were dangers on the ocean then which to-day we do not fear, for pirates still lay in wait for merchantmen and foreign powers took liberties with American ships. One vessel seen in Boston harbor was named *Catch-me-if-you-can*.

Many years later, when Mr. Samuel Cunard of Halifax took a contract to carry the royal mail between Liverpool and America, there was an immediate protest from the Boston merchants against ending the voyage at Halifax. They urged the great commercial advantage of having the ships run westward to Boston after stopping at Halifax, and so powerful were these arguments that the first Cunard liners came steaming into Massachusetts bay.

This was not pleasant for New York people, who tried to show that theirs was the better port. As if to help in the fight against Boston, the harbor froze over

FIG. 1. ONE OF THE CUNARD STEAMSHIPS WHICH SAIL FROM BOSTON TO-DAY

in the winter of 1844, and the Cunard ship, the *Britannia*, could not sail. Determined to hold their own, the Boston people engaged Frederick Tudor, a great exporter of ice, to bring his machinery from the freshwater ponds and cut a way. He soon made a lane of open water, and the *Britannia* sailed out for Liverpool.

While ocean trade was growing much had been done on the land. Settlements were first made at Plymouth, Salem, and Boston, and as soon as possible the rough forest trails joining these towns were changed into roads. Many ferries and bridges were needed to cross the streams, and roads were carried back into the country as the people settled farther from the sea.

After Providence was begun, in the Narragansett country, and the rich lands along the Connecticut were settled, there was need of roads across the hills of Massachusetts, so that the colonists could visit each other, exchange letters, and thus be less exposed to danger from savages in the great American wilderness.

The highway leading along the east coast was called Bay Road. A post rider went between Boston and New York in 1704, and a rough path he had to travel. It was thought remarkable, four years later, that a woman, Madam Sarah Knights, made that journey. She afterwards taught school in Boston, and Benjamin Franklin was one of her pupils. Somebody scratched these lines on a window pane in her schoolroom:

> Through many toils and many frights
> I have returned, poor Sarah Knights;
> Over great rocks and many stones,
> God has preserved from fractured bones.

BOSTON AND MAINE RAILROAD (FITCHBURG DIVISION) ••••••••••
BOSTON AND ALBANY RAILROAD ―――――

There is no doubt about the "great rocks and many stones" of New England, but around Boston, at any rate, one usually sees them now at a safe distance.

In western Massachusetts is the great Berkshire country. Through most of its length the Housatonic river runs to the southward. At the north the Hoosick river flows from it, across a corner of Vermont, to the Hudson. On the first is beautiful Pittsfield, and on the second is busy North Adams with its mills. In sight everywhere are the mountains, not very high and usually covered with forest, but sometimes bold and rocky. Farther north we should call them the Green mountains, but here we name them the Berkshires. The eastern range, which separates the Housatonic valley on the west from the Connecticut valley on the east, is Hoosac mountain, of which we shall hear again.

These long ranges of mountains run from north to south, and while it was easy to follow the valleys between them, it was hard to go across them from east to west or from west to east. Boston and all the chief towns of New England lay eastward, and the rest of the country was west of the mountains. If a Massachusetts family wished to settle in the fertile lands of western New York or Ohio, they had to cross the mountains. In our day the mountain region is full of towns and beautiful summer homes, but then it was a wilderness which in places was almost impassable. If it was difficult to make a single journey between the Connecticut river and the Hudson, it was quite out of the question to carry grain and fruit from the West to Boston, and to bring back in exchange the goods made in her factories.

6 FROM TRAIL TO RAILWAY

Near Pittsfield, in the heart of the Berkshires, rises the Westfield river, which has cut a deep valley eastward through the mountains. Opposite the place where this stream enters the Connecticut the beautiful city of Springfield has now grown up, partly on the low grounds and partly on a terrace. It is readily seen that the Westfield valley forms a natural roadway from here westward

FIG. 2. UNION RAILWAY STATION, SPRINGFIELD, MASSACHUSETTS

to Pittsfield, and on toward Albany and the Mohawk in New York. We cannot say that the valley was made for the cities, but the cities were made, in part at least, because the valley was there.

The first roads that improved on the Indian trails were, of course, made for wagons. The gorge of the Westfield was so rugged that a hundred years ago it seemed almost impossible to make a good wagon road through it. There were some people, however, who thought that it could be done and who determined to do it. Their courage won, and before long there was a good highway all along the roaring river. The bowlders were rolled out of the way, the trees were cut, the road-bed was made, and people could go east and west in the stages without risk of losing their lives or even of breaking their bones. This was accomplished soon after 1825, but it did not solve all the problems of the Massachusetts people, for, as we shall soon learn fully, the Erie canal was finished in that year, and a long string of canal boats began to carry produce from the West to New York.

The good people of Boston watched all this going on. Every load of grain was headed straight eastward as if it were coming to Massachusetts bay, thence to go by vessel to Europe. But when it reached the Hudson it was sure to turn off down that river to help load ships at the piers of New York. And New England had only a wagon road across the mountains! A wagon road will never draw trade away from a tidal river, and thus we can understand why a prominent Massachusetts man, Charles Francis Adams, spoke of the Hudson as "a river so fatal to Boston." Boston might have all the ships she wanted, but if she could not get cargoes for them they would be of no use. Shipowners, seeing that there was plenty of western freight in New York, sent their boats there. It was indeed time that Boston people began to ask themselves what they could do.

They still had ships, but these were usually "down East" coasters, and the noble vessels from far eastern

8   FROM TRAIL TO RAILWAY

ports, laden with spices and teas, silks, and all the spoils of Europe and Asia, rarely came to Boston, but brought more and greater loads to New York and Baltimore, where they could lay in corn and wheat for the return voyage. Even the Cunards transferred most of their boats and finally all their mail steamers to New York.

The people of Boston first said, "We will build another canal, up the Hoosick and down the Deerfield valley, and then the canal boats will keep on to the east."

Fig. 3. The Valley of Deerfield River at Charlemont, Massachusetts, on the Line of the Boston and Maine Railroad

As states often do, they appointed a commission to see if the canal could be built, and what it would cost. But what were they to do about Hoosac mountain, which stood a thousand feet high, of solid rock, between the Hoosick valley on the west and the Deerfield valley on the east?

They decided that they would tunnel it for the water way. Rather strangely they thought it could be done for a little less than a million dollars. A wise engineer made the survey for the canal, and when he remarked, "It seems as if the finger of Providence had pointed out this route from the east to the west," some one who stood near replied, "It's a great pity that the same finger was n't thrust through the mountain." The plans for the canal were finally given up, and though many years later such a tunnel was made, it was not for a canal, nor was the work done for a million dollars.

Every one was talking now of railways, but few thought that rails could be laid across the Berkshires. It was even said in a Boston paper that such a road could never be built to Albany; that it would cost as much to do it as all Massachusetts would sell for; and that if it should be finished, everybody with common sense knew it would be as useless as a railroad from Boston to the moon. We need not be too hard on this writer, for it was five years later when the De Witt Clinton train climbed the hill from Albany and carried its handful of passengers to Schenectady.

One of the friends of the railway scheme was Abner Phelps. When he was a senior at Williams College, in 1806, he had thought of it, for he had heard about the tram cars in the English coal regions. In 1826 he became a member of the legislature of Massachusetts, and the second day he was there he proposed that the road should be built.

In time the project went through, but at first it was planned to pull the cars with horses, and on the down grades to take the horses on the cars and let them ride. We do not know how it was intended that the cars should be held back, for it was long before the invention of air brakes. The line was built to its western end on the Hudson in 1842, and thus Boston, Worcester, Springfield, and Albany were bound together by iron rails.

There was only a single track and the grades were heavy. The road brought little trade to Boston, and most of the goods from the West still went by way of the Hudson to New York. It was, however, a beginning, and it showed that the mountain wall could be crossed.

The subject of a Hoosac tunnel now came up again. It would take a long time to tell how the tunnel was made; indeed, it was a long time in making. It was begun in 1850 or soon afterwards, and the work went slowly, with many stops and misfortunes, so that the hole through the mountain was not finished until November 27, 1873. On that day the last blast was set off, which made the opening from the east to the west side, and the first regular passenger train ran through July 8, 1875, fifty years after it had been planned to make a canal under the mountain.

In order to help on the work the engineers sunk a shaft a thousand feet deep from the top of the mountain to the level of the tunnel, and from the bottom worked east and west. This gave them four faces, or "headings," on which to work, instead of two, and hastened the finishing. The whole cost was about fourteen million dollars.

It took great skill to sink the shaft on just the right line, and to make the parts of the tunnel exactly meet,

Fig. 4. Eastern Portal of the Hoosac Tunnel, Boston and Maine Railroad

as the men worked in from opposite directions. They brought the ends together under the mountain with a difference of only five sixteenths of an inch! You can measure this on a finger nail and see how much it is. The tremendous task was successfully accomplished, and Boston was no longer shut off from the rest of the country by the mountains.

The end of it all is not that Boston has won all the ships away from New York, but that gradually she has

FIG. 5. THE SOUTH STATION, BOSTON

been getting her share. Now she has great Cunarders, White Star Liners, and the Leyland boats,—all giant ships sailing for Liverpool,—and many other stately vessels bound for southern ports or foreign lands. Now you may see in Boston harbor not a forest of masts but great funnels painted to show the lines to which the boats belong, and marking a grander commerce than that which put out for the Indies long years ago; for to-day Boston is the second American port. The great freight yards of the railways are close upon the docks, and travelers from the West may come into either of two great stations, one of which is the largest railway terminal in the world. In and about Boston are more than a million people, reaching out with one hand for the riches of the great land to the west, and with the other passing them over the seas to the nations on the farther side.

Man has taken a land of dense forests, stony hills, and wild valleys, and subdued it. It is dotted with cities, crossed by roads, and is one of the great gateways of North America.

CHAPTER II

PIONEERS OF THE MOHAWK AND THE HUDSON

If a stranger from a distant land should come to New York, he might take an elevated train at the Battery and ride to the upper end of Harlem. He would then have seen Manhattan island, so named by the Indians, who but three hundred years ago built their wigwams there and paddled their canoes in the waters where great ships now wait for their cargoes. If the visitor should stay for a time, he might find that Harlem used to be spelled Haarlem, from a famous old town in Holland. He might walk through Bleecker street, or Cortlandt street, or see Stuyvesant square, and learn that these hard names belonged to old Dutch families; and if he studied history, he would find that the town was once called New Amsterdam and was settled by Dutchmen from Holland. They named the river on the west of the island the Great North river, to distinguish it from the Delaware, or Great South river, and they planned to keep all the land about these two streams and to call it New Netherland.

Rocks and trees covered most of Manhattan island at that time, but the Dutch had a small village at its south end, where they built a fort and set up windmills, which ground the corn and made the place look like a town in

Holland. The Indians did not like the windmills with their "big teeth biting the corn in pieces," but they were usually friendly with the settlers, sometimes sitting before the fireplaces in the houses and eating supawn, or mush and milk, with their white friends. Little did the Indian dream what a bargain he offered to the white man when he consented to sell the whole island for a sum equal to twenty-four dollars; and the Dutchman, to do him justice, was equally ignorant.

All this came about because Henry Hudson with a Dutch vessel, the *Half Moon*, had sailed into the harbor in 1609, and had explored the river for a long distance from its mouth. Hudson was an Englishman, but with most people he has had to pass for a Dutchman. He has come down in stories as Hendrick instead of Henry, no doubt because he commanded a ship belonging to a Dutch company, and because a Dutch colony was soon planted at the mouth of the river which he discovered.

Hudson spent a month of early autumn about Manhattan and on the river which afterwards took his name. Sailing was easy, for the channel is cut so deep into the land that the tides, which rise and fall on the ocean border by day and night, push far up the Hudson and make it like an inland sea. In what we call the Highlands Hudson found the river narrow, with rocky cliffs rising far above him. Beyond he saw lowlands covered with trees, and stretching west to the foot of the Catskill mountains. He went at least as far as the place where Albany now stands, but there he found the water shallow and turned his ship about, giving up the idea of reaching the Indies by going that way. He did not know that a few miles to the west a deep valley lies open through the mountains, a valley which is now full of busy people and is more important for travel and trade than a dozen northwest passages to China would be.

FIG. 6. HENRY HUDSON

It was not long before this valley which leads to the west was found, and by a real Dutchman. Only five years after Hudson's voyage Dutch traders built a fort near the spot where Albany now stands. Shortly afterwards, in 1624, the first settlers came and founded Fort Orange, which is now Albany. Arent Van Curler came over from Holland in 1630 and made his home near Fort Orange. He was an able man and became friendly with the Indians. They called him "Brother Corlear" and spoke of him as their "good friend." A few years ago a diary kept by Van Curler was found in an old Dutch garret, where it had lain for two hundred and sixty years. It told the story of a journey that he made in 1634, only four years after he came to America. Setting out on December 11, he traveled up the valley of the Mohawk until he reached the home of the Oneida Indians in central New York. He stayed with them nearly two weeks, and then returned to Fort Orange, where he arrived on January 19. This is the earliest record of a white man's journey through a region which now contains large towns and is traversed by many railway trains every day in the year.

No one knows how long there had been Indians and Indian trails in the Mohawk valley. These trails Van Curler followed, often coming upon some of the red men themselves, and visiting them in a friendly way. They, as well as the white settlers who followed them, chose the flat, rich lands along the river, for here it was easy to beat a path, and with their bark canoes they could travel and fish. The Indians entertained Van Curler with baked pumpkins, turkey, bear meat, and venison. As the turkey is an American bird, we may be sure that it was new to the Dutch explorer.

These Indians, with whom Van Curler and all the New York colonists had much to do, were of several tribes,

— the Mohawks, Oneidas, Onondagas, Cayugas, and Senecas. All together they were known as the Iroquois (ĭr-ŏ-kwoi'), or Iroquois Nation, a kind of confederation which met in council and went forth together to war. They called their five-fold league The Long House, from the style of dwelling which was common among them, — a long house in which as many as twenty families sometimes lived. The Iroquois built villages, cultivated plots of land, and sometimes planted apple orchards. They were often eloquent orators and always fierce fighters. Among the surrounding tribes they were greatly feared. They sailed on lake Ontario and lake Erie in their birch-bark canoes, and they followed the trails far eastward down the Mohawk valley. Before the white men came these fierce warriors occasionally invaded New England, to the terror of the weaker tribes. Sometimes they followed up their conquests by exacting a tribute of wampum. After Fort Orange was founded they went there with their packs of beaver skins and other furs to trade for clothes and trinkets.

In fact the white man's principal interest for many years was to barter for furs. The Dutch, and soon afterwards the English, bid for the trade from their settlements on the Hudson, and the French did the same from their forts on the St. Lawrence and the Great Lakes. Thus there was much letter writing and much fighting among the colonists, while each side tried to make friends of the Indians and get the whole of the fur trade. The result was that either in war or in trade the white men and the savages were always going up and down the Mohawk valley, which thus was a well-traveled path long before there were turnpike roads, canals, or steam cars.

When Van Curler made his journey into the Indian country, he did not reach the Mohawk river at once on leaving Fort Orange, but traveled for about sixteen miles across a sandy and half-barren stretch of scrubby pine woods. He came down to the river where its rich bottom lands spread out widely and where several large islands are inclosed by parts of the stream. South and east of these flats are the sand barrens, and on the west are high hills through which, by a deep, narrow gap, the Mohawk flows. The Indians called this place "Schonowe," or "gateway." It was well named, for entering by this gate one can go to the foot of the Rocky mountains without climbing any heights.

A few years before his death Van Curler led a small band of colonists from Fort Orange, bought the "great flats" from the Mohawk Indians, and founded a town, calling it Schenectady, which is the old Indian name changed in its spelling. No easy time did these settlers have, for theirs was for many years the frontier town and they never knew when hostile savages might come down upon them to burn their houses and take their scalps. In 1690, twenty-eight years after the town was founded, a company of French and Indians from Montreal surprised Schenectady in the night, burned most of the houses, and killed about sixty of the people, taking others captive. But Dutchmen rarely give up an undertaking, and they soon rebuilt their town. It was an important place, for here was the end of the "carry" over the pine barrens from the Hudson, and here began the navigation of the river, which for a hundred years was the best means of carrying supplies up the valley and into central New York.

The traveler of to-day on the New York Central Railway sees on Van Curler's "great flats" the flourishing city of Schenectady, with its shops and houses, its college, and its vast factories for the manufacture of locomotives and electrical supplies.

It is true that the Dutch pioneers played an important part in the early history of the state and are still widely represented by their descendants in the Mohawk valley, but the leading spirit of colonial days on the river was a native of Ireland who came when a young man to manage his uncle's estates in America. This was in 1738, nearly fifty years after the Schenectady massacre. The young man, who was in the confidence of the governor of New York and of the king as well, is known to all readers of American history as Sir William Johnson.

FIG. 7. SIR WILLIAM JOHNSON

See Fort Johnson, Fig. 9

He built a fine stone mansion a short distance west of the present city of Amsterdam and lived there many years. He also founded Johnstown, a few miles to the north, now a thriving little city. He dealt honestly with the Indians, when many tried to get their lands by fraud, and he served as a high officer in the French and Indian wars.

As the Dutch settled the lower Mohawk valley, so the upper parts were taken up and the forests cleared by Yankees from New England. One of these was Hugh White, a sturdy man with several grown children. He left Middletown, Connecticut, in 1784, and came by water to Albany, sending one of his sons overland to drive two pair of oxen. Father and son met in Albany and went together across the sands to Schenectady, where they bought a boat to take some of the goods up the river. Four miles west of where Utica now stands they stopped, cut a few trees, and built a hut to shelter them until they could raise crops and have a better home. Thus the ancient village of Whitesboro was founded. White was one of many hardy and brave men who settled in central New York at that time, and they doubtless thought that they had gone a long way "out West." Certainly their journey took more time than the emigrant would now need to reach California or Oregon.

To cut the trees, build cabins, guard against the savages, and get enough to eat and wear gave the settlers plenty to do. Only the simplest ways of living were possible. Until a grist mill was built they often used samp mortars, such as the Indians made. They took a section of white ash log three feet long, and putting coals of fire on one end, kept them burning with a hand bellows until the hole was deep enough to hold the corn, which was then pounded for their meals of hominy. By and by a mill was built, and here settlers often came from a distance of many miles, sometimes carrying their grists on their backs. A dozen years after White came, General William Floyd set up another mill in the northern part of what is now Oneida county. He was one of the signers of the Declaration of Independence.

One settler cleared several acres and planted corn with pumpkin seeds sprinkled in. The pigeons pulled up all the corn, but hundreds of great pumpkins grew and ripened. Since the crop was hardly enough, however, for either men or beasts, the latter had to be fed the next winter on the small top boughs of the elm, maple, and basswood.

Much use was made of the river, for the only roads were Indian paths through the woods on the river flats. People and freight were carried in long, light boats suited to river traffic and known as bateaux (bȧ-tōs′). These could be propelled with oars, but poles were necessary going upstream against a stiff current. It was impossible to go up the Mohawk from the Hudson above Albany, on account of the great falls at Cohoes; hence the long carry to Schenectady. From that place, by hard work, the boatmen could make their way up to Little Falls, where the water descends forty feet in roaring rapids. Here the loads and the bateaux had to be carried along the banks to the still water above, where, with many windings and doublings on their course, the voyagers could reach the Oneida Carrying Place, or Fort Stanwix. There they unloaded again, and for a mile or more tramped across low ground to Wood creek, a little stream flowing into Oneida lake, and thence into Oswego river and lake Ontario. The city of Rome stands exactly on the road followed by the "carry." This was an important place, and was called by the Dutch Trow Plat, while to the Indians it was De-o-wain-sta, "the place where canoes are carried across." Several forts were built there, of which the most famous was Fort Stanwix. We should think Wood creek a difficult bit of navigation. It was a small stream, very crooked, and

FIG. 8. GENESEE STREET, UTICA
Part of the old Genesee road

often interrupted by fallen trees. In times of low water the boats were dragged up and even down the creek by horses walking in the water.

The first merchant of old Fort Schuyler (Utica) was John Post, who had served his country well through the Revolution. In 1790 he brought hither his wife, three little children, and a carpenter from Schenectady, after a voyage of about nine days up the river. Near the long-used fording place he built a store, at the foot of what is now Genesee street. Here he supplied the simple needs of the few families in the new hamlet, and bought furs and ginseng of the Indians, giving in exchange paint, powder, shot, cloth, beads, mirrors, and, it must be added, rum also. Thus the fact that the river was shallow at this point and could be passed without a bridge or a boat led to the founding of the city of Utica.

The first regular mail reached the settlement in 1793, the post rider being allowed twenty-eight hours to come up from Canajoharie, a distance of about forty miles, now traversed by many trains in much less than an hour. On one occasion the Fort Schuyler settlement received six letters in one mail. The people would hardly believe this astonishing fact until John Post, who had been made postmaster, assured them that it was true. Post established stages and lines of boats to Schenectady, and soon had a large business, for people were pouring into western New York to settle upon its fertile lands.

All the boats did not go down to Oswego and lake Ontario. Some turned and entered the Seneca river, following its slow and winding waters to the country now lying between Syracuse and Rochester. But these boats were not equal to the traffic, for the new farms were producing grain to be transported, and the people needed many articles from the older towns on the Atlantic coast. Hence about a dozen years after Hugh White built his first cabin by the river, the state legislature took up the question of transportation and built a great road, a hundred miles long, from Fort Schuyler, or the future Utica, to Geneva, at the foot of Seneca lake.

PIONEERS OF THE MOHAWK AND HUDSON 25

The road as laid out was six rods wide. It was improved for a width of four rods by the use of gravel and logs where the ground was soft and swampy, as much of it was in those days, being flat and shaded by trees. Over the famous Genesee road, as it was called, thousands of people went not only to the rich valley of the Genesee in western New York but also on to Ohio, and even to the prairies of the Mississippi river. Genesee street in Utica and Genesee street in Syracuse are parts of this road. The historian tells of it as a triumph, for it was an Indian path in June, and before September was over a stage had started at Fort Schuyler, and on the afternoon of the third day had deposited its four passengers at the hotel in Geneva. After this wagons and stages began to run frequently between Albany and Geneva. A wagon could carry fourteen barrels of flour eastward, and in about a month could return to Geneva from Albany with a load of needed supplies. In five weeks, one winter, five hundred and seventy sleighs carrying families passed through Geneva to lands farther west.

Geneva was quite a metropolis in those days, when there was nothing but woods where Syracuse and Rochester now are. Regular markets were held there, for there were fine farms and orchards about the beautiful shores of Seneca lake. It is recorded as remarkable that one settler had "dressed up" an old Indian orchard and made "one hundred barrels of cyder."

We might think that the founders of the city of Rochester would have come in by the Genesee road, but they did not. Far to the south, at Hagerstown in

Maryland, a country already old, lived Colonel Rochester. He heard of the Genesee lands and at last bought, with his partners, a hundred acres by the falls, where the city now stands. When the little family procession passed down the street and entered upon the long journey up the Susquehanna valley to western New York, Rochester's friends in Hagerstown wept to see him go. They

FIG. 9. OLD FORT JOHNSON, AMSTERDAM, NEW YORK
Built by Sir William Johnson, 1742

thought that he had thrown his money away in buying swamp lands where only mosquitoes, rattlesnakes, and bears could live, but he saw farther than they did. If he had been unwilling to take any risk, he would never have laid out the first streets of the prosperous city which now bears his name.

Syracuse, like Utica and Rochester, had its own way of beginning. We can truly say that at first salt made

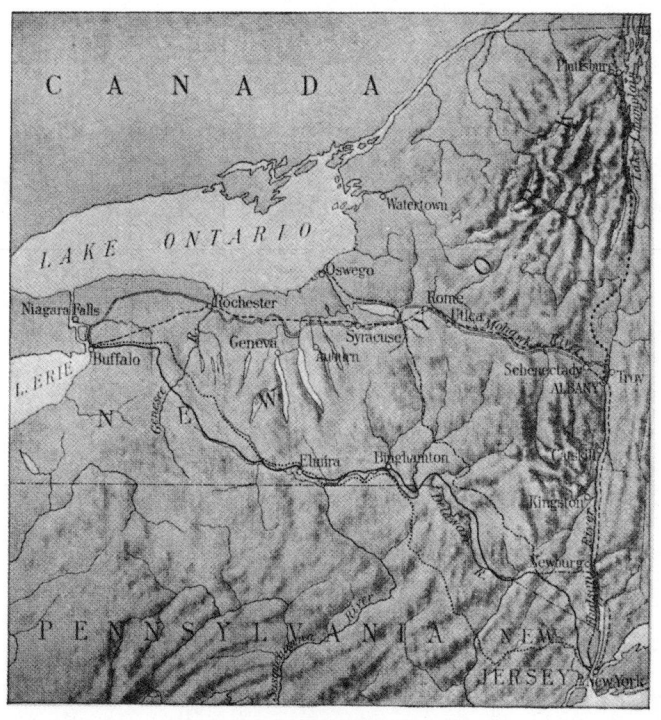

NEW YORK, LAKE ERIE AND WESTERN RAILROAD ———
DELAWARE, LACKAWANNA AND WESTERN RAILROAD ············
NEW YORK CENTRAL AND HUDSON RIVER RAILROAD ----------
NEW YORK, ONTARIO AND WESTERN RAILROAD —·—·—·—·—
DELAWARE AND HUDSON RAILROAD ++++++++++
ERIE CANAL (old location) ══════

the city. The beds of salt are not directly under Syracuse, but are in the hills not far away. The water from the rains and springs dissolves some of this salt, and as it flows down it fills the gravels in and around the town. While all was yet forest the Indian women had made salt from the brine which oozed up in the springs. So long ago as 1770, five years before the Revolution, the Delaware Indians went after Onondaga salt, and a little of it was now and then brought down to Albany. Sometimes it was sold far down the St. Lawrence in Quebec.

The pioneers first made salt there in 1788. This was several years before the Genesee road was cut through the woods. One of these men, a Mr. Danforth, whose name a suburb of Syracuse now bears, used to put his coat on his head for a cushion and on that carry out a large kettle to the springs. He would put a pole across crotched sticks, hang up the kettle, and go to work to make salt. When he had made enough for the time he would hide his kettle in the bushes and bring home his salt. By and by so many hundreds of bushels were made by the settlers that the government of the state framed laws to regulate the making and selling of the salt, and as time went on a town arose and grew into a city. Many years later rock salt was found deep down under the surface farther west, and since that discovery the business of Syracuse has become more and more varied in character.

The history of the state of New York shows well how the New World was settled along the whole Atlantic coast. The white men from Europe found first Manhattan island and the harbor. Then they followed the lead of a river and made a settlement that was to be Albany. Still they let a river guide them, this time the Mohawk, and it led them westward. They pushed their boats up the stream, and on land they widened the trails of the red men. Near its head the Mohawk valley led out into the wide, rich plains south and east of lake Ontario. Soon there were so many people that a good road became necessary. When the good road was made it brought more people, and thus the foundations of the Empire State were laid.

CHAPTER III

ORISKANY, A BATTLE OF THE REVOLUTION

About halfway between old Fort Schuyler, or Utica, and Fort Stanwix, which is now Rome, is the village of Oriskany. A mile or two west of this small town, in a field south of the Mohawk river, stands a monument raised in memory of a fierce battle fought on that slope in the year following the Declaration of Independence. On the pedestal are four tablets in bronze, one of which shows a wounded general sitting on the ground in the woods, with his hand raised, giving orders to his men. The time was 1777, the strife was the battle of Oriskany, and the brave and suffering general was Nicholas Herkimer.

On another of the tablets is this inscription:

> HERE WAS FOUGHT
> THE BATTLE OF ORISKANY
> ON THE 6TH DAY OF AUGUST, 1777.
> HERE BRITISH INVASION WAS CHECKED AND THWARTED.
> HERE GENERAL NICHOLAS HERKIMER,
> INTREPID LEADER OF THE AMERICAN FORCES,
> THOUGH MORTALLY WOUNDED KEPT HIS COMMAND OF THE FIGHT
> TILL THE ENEMY HAD FLED.
> THE LIFE BLOOD OF MORE THAN
> TWO HUNDRED PATRIOT HEROES
> MADE THIS BATTLE GROUND
> SACRED FOREVER.

After the battle Herkimer was carried down the valley to his home, where a few days later he died. On the field he had calmly lighted his pipe and smoked it as he gave his orders, refusing to be carried to a safe place and saying, "I will face the enemy." If the battle has its monument, so the hero that won it has his, and the traveler on the New York Central Railway can

Fig. 10. Oriskany Battle Monument, a Few Miles West of Utica

see both, but thirty miles apart, the one at Oriskany, the other a short distance down the valley from Little Falls.

Herkimer was not a trained soldier, but a plain farmer of the valley. His letters and military orders show us that he could spell as poorly as any of his neighbors, and that is saying a good deal. His army was made up of these same simple neighbors, who, though they did not know much about soldierly marching, were good shots and hard hitters, fighting not for pay but to save their liberty and to protect their homes from the cruel savages.

The names of many of these men are on the battle monument, — names such as Groot, Petrie, Dunckel, Klock, Kraus, Sammons, Schnell, Van Horn, and Zimmerman. We do not need to be told that these were not men of English blood; indeed, many of them belonged to those same Dutch families which we saw settling in the Hudson and Mohawk valleys. And some, like the last one, were not Dutch but German, and their ancestors came not from Holland but from a land farther up the Rhine. They had been driven out by the persecutions of one of the French kings and had come to America. They had had a hard time, suffering much from taskmasters, from poverty, and from the savages, until finally they had gone farther west in the Mohawk valley and had received good lands lying eastward from Utica. There they became comfortable and prosperous. They answered promptly the brave Herkimer's call to arms, and many of them gave their lives for home and country at Oriskany.

We must now tell the other side of the story and see who the invaders were and where they came from. In Revolutionary days nearly all the people of New York were in its two great valleys. One could go up the Hudson from New York, pass Albany and Fort Edward, and, without finding high ground, enter the valley of lake Champlain and go down to Montreal on the St. Lawrence. Here, then, was an easy valley road from the sea at New York into Canada. Coming either way, one could turn off to the west at Fort

Orange or Albany and go up the Mohawk and down to Oswego on lake Ontario. In these two valleys were all the farms, the towns, and of course the forts. There were forts at Oswego and where Rome, Utica, and Albany are; at Fort Edward, Fort Ann, Ticonderoga, and many other places, making a chain of defenses in these valleys. West of the Hudson and south of the Mohawk were the high, rough woods of the Catskills; while west of lake Champlain and north of the Mohawk were the rugged Adirondacks, without roads or clearings. And because the roads, the homes, and the forts were in the valleys, we shall almost always find the armies and the fighting there.

This will help us to understand the plan which the British made in 1777, by which they felt sure of crushing the rebellion. The year before they had to leave Boston and had come around to New York. New York was not so large as Philadelphia then, but it was an important place, for it was the key to the Hudson valley. The British generals decided to send one army up the Hudson to destroy the forts and beat back the colonists. This army was under General Howe. Another army, commanded by General Burgoyne, was to come from the St. Lawrence up lake Champlain and through the woods by Fort Edward to Albany. Burgoyne was a brave officer, but he was conceited, and he felt too sure that he could do his part easily. He was confident that when he marched through the country many colonists would run to place themselves under the English flag. In a few weeks he learned that these backwoods Americans were quite ready to meet and give battle to the

ORISKANY, A BATTLE OF THE REVOLUTION 33

combined forces of the British regulars, the hired German soldiers, and the Indians with whom they were in league.

There was yet a third division in this campaign. A British force under General St. Leger had come up the St. Lawrence and lake Ontario to Oswego. St. Leger

FIG. 11. GENERAL NICHOLAS HERKIMER DIRECTING THE BATTLE OF ORISKANY

also had with him many Indians, and these were commanded by Joseph Brant, a famous chief, who had had much to do with white men and who was well educated. This third army was to go east, over the Oneida Carrying Place and down the Mohawk to Albany. By this pretty plan three armies, one from the south under Howe, one from the north under Burgoyne, and one from the west under St. Leger, were to meet in Albany. They would put British soldiers in every fort on the way, capture and disarm the rebels, and have all New York under their feet. More than this, they would thus shut off New England from Pennsylvania and Virginia, cutting the unruly colonies into two parts so that they could not help each other.

But the scheme, brilliant as it was, would not work. None of the British armies reached Albany. Howe did not, perhaps because he did not try. Burgoyne and St. Leger did not, because they could not: there was altogether too much in the way. We shall now see how this happened.

St. Leger brought into the Mohawk valley from Oswego an army of seventeen hundred men. Some were British, some were Hessians or hired German soldiers, and the rest were Indians under Joseph Brant. They thought that it would not be much trouble to take Fort Stanwix and then go down the valley, burning and killing as they went, until they should meet the other armies of the king at Albany. But the colonists sent more soldiers to defend the fort, and Colonel Peter Gansevoort, who was in command, had under him nearly a thousand men. Just before the British came in sight a stock of provisions, brought on several boats up the river, had been safely delivered within the defenses. This was early in August, and only about seven weeks before Congress had adopted the style of American flag which we know so well. There was no flag at Fort Stanwix, so the garrison set about making one. They cut up shirts to make the white. The blue came from a

ORISKANY, A BATTLE OF THE REVOLUTION 35

cloak captured not long before in a battle, on the Hudson, by Colonel Marinus Willett, one of the bravest commanders within the fort. The red is said to have been taken from a petticoat. Certain it is that a patriot flag was made, and some think that it was the first American flag ever raised over a fortification.

While the British were besieging Fort Stanwix, General Herkimer had called out the men of the valley, bidding all between the ages of sixteen and sixty make ready for battle. The boys and old men were to do their best to care for the families and to defend their homes. Eight hundred men gathered under Herkimer and marched to help the garrison of the fort. Hearing of this, part of the British army, including the Indians, came down the valley to head off Herkimer. They met at Oriskany. The farmer soldiers were hurrying up the valley without due watching for sudden attack, while the enemy placed themselves in ambush around a low field which was wooded and swampy. Through this field the road ran, and when Herkimer's men were well down into it the Indians opened a hot fire, which threw the patriots into disorder. They soon rallied and fought fiercely for five hours, until two hundred of them had lost their lives. Early in the battle Herkimer was shot, but he forgot his pain when he saw his men victorious. Much of the fighting was of the Indian sort, from behind trees, for the Dutchmen well knew the ways of the savages. They saw that when one man fired from behind a tree an Indian would rush forward to tomahawk him before he could load his gun for another shot. So they were ordered to stand by twos and take turns in firing. Thus when the Indian ran forward with his tomahawk he would receive a bullet from the other man's gun.

Under John Johnson, the son of Sir William Johnson, were many Tories from the valley. They and the patriots often recognized each other as former neighbors, and then the fight was more stubborn than ever, for the soldiers of freedom were bitterly angry to find old

FIG. 12. NICHOLAS HERKIMER'S MONUMENT
To the right is the old mansion in which he lived. Near Little Falls, New York

friends in arms against them. During the battle a terrific thunder-shower came up, and both sides stopped fighting, having enough to do to keep their powder and guns dry. The dark storm passed and the strife went on again. At length the Indians grew tired and ran, leaving the field to Herkimer and his little army. The importance of a conflict is not always in proportion to the size of the armies engaged, and in what it did for freedom Oriskany takes high place among the battles of modern times.

The enemy went back to the siege of Fort Stanwix, and soon a new force of patriots under Benedict Arnold was sent up the valley to relieve the fort. It was during this march that an ignorant but cunning fellow named Han Yost Schuyler was caught, tried, and condemned to die as a spy. Because his friends pleaded for his life Arnold finally told him that he might live if he would go up to Fort Stanwix and make the Indians and British believe that a great army was marching against them. Meanwhile the man's brother was held as a hostage, to be punished if the promise was not fulfilled. Han Yost did his part so well that St. Leger, taking fright, left the fort in great haste and his expedition was entirely broken up. Why he did not have a gay march down to Albany is now quite plain.

A few days after the battle of Oriskany a number of men drove some cattle to Fort Stanwix as food for the soldiers. Several women went with them on horseback to visit their husbands, who belonged to the garrison. At the ford of the river, now the Genesee street crossing in Utica, a big Dutchman, who did not wish to get wet, leaped uninvited upon a horse behind one of the women. The horse did not like the double load, and made great sport by throwing the Dutchman into the middle of the stream, while he carried his mistress over in safety.

General Burgoyne came nearer Albany than did St. Leger. Indeed he went to Albany, but not until he had lost his army. He had promptly captured Ticonderoga on lake Champlain, and this success gave him high hopes and sent rejoicing throughout Great Britain; but the patriots, by felling trees and cutting away bridges, hindered his southward march in every way. He sent a thousand of his German soldiers across to Bennington, among the Green mountains, to capture stores which he knew were there. But General Stark was there also, with a little army from New Hampshire and Massachusetts, and the thousand Hessians did not go back to help Burgoyne. He had left another thousand to guard Ticonderoga, and so he was two thousand short. All this time the patriot army was growing, for the men of the Hudson valley were maddened when they saw the bloodthirsty Indians marching with the English, and, to Burgoyne's surprise, they had no mind to fight for the king. Howe did not come, St. Leger did not come, and the provisions were getting short. These could only come along the road from the north, and the colonists were already marching in behind Burgoyne's army to cut his line of communications. He knew that he must fight or starve. He chose to fight. The battle was fought on Bemis Heights, a range of hills west of the Hudson, a short distance north of the little village of Stillwater. The British general, after his defeat, withdrew a few miles northward and surrendered his army near the present town of Schuylerville. A tall monument marks the place. This was the battle of Saratoga, fought in old Saratoga, which is several miles from the famous resort of that name.

So it was that up and down these beautiful valleys went armies and scouting bands, as well as peaceful emigrants with their oxen, their stages, and their small freight boats. One cannot go far along the Hudson or the Mohawk without finding the site of an Indian village, the foundations of an old fort, the homestead of a Revolutionary hero, or an ancient place of worship. When we see the great railways and swift trains, the bundles of telegraph wires, the noisy cities and great mills of to-day, we can remember Philip Schuyler, Sir William Johnson, Marinus Willett, Peter Gansevoort, and Nicholas Herkimer. There were no nobler patriots, even in Virginia and Massachusetts, than these men of the Mohawk valley.

CHAPTER IV

THE ERIE CANAL

If we think that the men of a hundred years ago were people with few wants, who were willing to let others do the trading and make the fortunes, we are quite in the wrong. They were as eager in business as are the driving Americans of to-day. So long ago as 1683 Thomas Dongan, a well-born Irishman, came to New York to be its governor. In his letters to the government in London he said a great deal about the fur trade and the danger of its going to other cities. Once he reported that two hundred packs of beaver skins had gone down the Susquehanna river and across to Philadelphia instead of being brought by the Mohawk to New York, and he thought that if this traffic continued New York would be ruined.

As time went on the rivalry grew stronger and stronger. All the cities on the coast were bidding for the western trade. The "West" was then the Genesee country, the plains along the Lakes, and the rich lands of the Ohio valley. Some of the trade from the Lakes and the Genesee went down the St. Lawrence. Heavy articles especially were sent to Quebec, while lighter freight was taken overland down the Mohawk. When De Witt Clinton was stirring up the legislature and the people of New York, he told them he was very sorry to learn that merchandise from Montreal was sold in the state for less than New York prices. This was because there was transportation by water from Montreal, and the St. Lawrence merchants could afford to undersell those of New York.

Many people thought that the wheat and flour and other products of western New York would all go down the Susquehanna to Baltimore and Philadelphia. Rough boats known as "arks" were built and floated down the river in the high water caused by the melting of the snows in the Allegheny highlands. From two to five hundred barrels of flour were carried in one of these craft. As the boats could not be sailed up the river, they were taken to pieces at the end of the voyage and sold for lumber. We have already seen that Colonel Rochester followed this valley in migrating to the Genesee river, and one writer calls attention to the fact that in seven days several elderly people had come quite comfortably by this route from Baltimore to Bath in the southwestern part of New York. One could now travel from San Francisco to New York and almost halfway across the Atlantic ocean in that time.

Other cities also hoped to secure some of the profits of dealing with the rapidly growing West. The tourist on his way down the Potomac to Mount Vernon, the home of Washington, will pass by Alexandria, a quiet old town of about fifteen thousand people. Washington himself thought it possible that Alexandria might get a good share of the trade from Detroit and other places on the Lakes and on the Ohio river. All this seems strange to us, because since the days of our great-grandfathers the traffic has been going largely to New York. The cause of the change was the Erie canal. Yet in 1818, a few months after the canal was begun, an Albany newspaper discussed very earnestly, as one of the chief questions of the day, the danger that Philadelphia would take away the western trade.

Flour, salt, and potash had been taken to New York in large quantities, but all these products were carried as far as Schenectady in little ten-ton boats, by way of Wood creek and the Mohawk. As the business grew it was seen to be impossible always to drag the boats up Wood creek with horses, and that the small canal, ten feet wide, which had been cut around the rapids at Little Falls, could not serve the purposes of another generation.

Hence for many years there had been talk of a canal to join the Lakes and the Hudson, thus making navigation without a break from the interior of the country to the Atlantic ocean at New York. The credit for first thinking of such a canal has been claimed for several men, but probably it was "in the air," and many thought of it at about the same time.

Gouverneur Morris, one of the famous New York statesmen of the day, proposed that lake Erie should be "tapped" and its waters led to the Hudson. The surface of this lake is five hundred and seventy-three feet above tide water at Albany. It was Morris's idea to dig a channel, with a gently sloping bottom, which should send the water east in a stream deep enough to float a boat. The water thus turned from its course would go to Albany instead of flowing through the Niagara

THE ERIE CANAL 43

and the St. Lawrence. There were, however, difficulties about the plan which Morris did not understand, and it was never carried out.

The great water way is often known as "Clinton's Ditch." This name was doubtless given in ridicule by

Fig. 13. De Witt Clinton

those who did not think it could be built. There were many who laughed at the surveyors when they saw them looking about, using their levels, and driving their stakes in the woods and swamps. It was even said that to dig such a canal was impossible, that it would cost too much money, that it would take too much time, and that the canal itself could never be made to hold water.

But Clinton and his supporters believed in it, and worked hard to make it a success. They said that the cost of carrying a ton of produce in wagons a distance of one hundred miles was about thirty-two dollars. The experience of others had proved that in canals a ton could be carried one mile for one cent, or a hundred miles for one dollar. There is a great difference between one dollar and thirty-two dollars, especially if the difference is added to the cost of the wheat from which our bread is made, or of the lumber used in building our houses. Clinton himself thought that it might take ten or fifteen years to make the canal, but, as we shall see, it was finished in less time than he supposed.

Clinton declared very truly that New York was especially fortunate, for the surface made it an easy task to dig the ditch. There was no high or rough ground to be crossed, there was plenty of water to keep the canal full, and it would run through a fertile and rich country. As Clinton was governor of New York during much of the period in which the canal was made, his name is imperishably connected with the great enterprise. He was once candidate for the office of President of the United States, but perhaps even that office, if he had been elected, would not have given him so much honor as did the building of this great public work.

Canals were not new in Clinton's time. Long before the Christian era began men had dug them to carry water for various uses, such as irrigation and turning machinery. Often, as for hundreds of years in the fen country of England, canals have been used to drain wet or flooded lands and for moving boats. Even beavers have been known to dig ditches, which fill with water, that they may float the wood which they cut to the place where they build their dams and their homes.

If a region is perfectly level, only a ditch and water are needed. But lands are not often level for more than short distances; hence a canal consists commonly of a series of levels at different heights. Of course the boats must be passed from one level to another by some means. If they are small, they can be dragged up or down between two levels; but this method will not serve for large boats carrying many tons of coal, lumber, salt, or bricks, hence locks are generally used. A lock is a short section of a canal, long enough for the boats used, and having walls rising from the bottom of the lower level to the top of the upper one. There are big gates at each end. If a boat is to ascend, it runs into the lock on the lower level and the lower gates are closed. A small gate in the large upper gate is then opened and the water runs in from above, slowly raising the water in the lock and with it the boat. When the water in the lock is even with the water in the upper level, the big upper gates are swung open and the boat goes on its way. In a similar manner boats go down from higher to lower sections of the canal. Locks have been used in Italy and in Holland for more than four hundred years.

On April 15, 1817, the legislature passed the law for the construction of the long ditch, and the first spade was set into the earth by Judge John Richardson at Rome, New York, on July 4 of the same year. This was forty-one years after the Declaration of Independence, and it is plain that the country had grown much in wealth and numbers when a single state could start out to build a water way three hundred miles long.

FIG. 14. ERIE CANAL, LOOKING EAST FROM GENESEE STREET BRIDGE, UTICA

After the first spadeful of soil had been lifted, the citizens and the laborers eagerly seized the shovels, and thus everybody had a small share in beginning the great work. Guns were fired and there was much rejoicing.

The men who took the contracts for digging short sections of the canal were mainly farmers who had gained good properties and who were living along the line. In those days, if any one had visited the men at work, he would not have seen crowds of foreign laborers living in huts, but men born and reared in the country round about. It was little more than twenty years since the Genesee road had been built through central New York, and there was still much forest. The trees grew rank and strong, and it was no light task to cut through the tangled network of roots that lay below the surface. First the trees were cut down, making a lane sixty feet wide, and in this the canal was dug to a width of forty feet. Powerful machines that could draw out stumps and pull over the largest trees were brought from Europe. The wheels of the stump machine were sixteen feet across. A plow with a sharp blade was also made, to cut down through the heavy carpet of fibers and small roots.

Swiftly one piece after another of the canal was finished and the water let in. The trench was found to hold water, and boats were soon busy hauling produce from town to town. In 1825 it was finished from Black Rock, or Buffalo, to Waterford, above Troy. The work had taken eight years and had cost a little less than eight million dollars. De Witt Clinton was right and the croakers were wrong. Perhaps it was hard at that time to find any one who did not think that he had always wanted a canal.

There were, it is true, a few disappointed ones at Schenectady. There the wagons from Albany had always stopped, and there the boating up the Mohawk had begun. As all the loads had to be shifted between the river and the land journeys, there had been work for many men. Thus the place had grown up, and now that boats were to run through without change, some people naturally thought that the town would die out, or would at least lose much of its business. These few discontented folk, however, were hardly to be counted, among the thousands who exulted over the completed canal.

A great celebration was arranged, and the rejoicings of the beginning were redoubled in the festivities at the end. Boats were made ready at Buffalo to take Governor Clinton and the other guests to New York.

FIG. 15. ALONG THE CANAL IN SYRACUSE
Copyrighted, 1899, by A. P. Yates, Syracuse, N.Y.

When the first boat entered the canal from lake Erie a cannon was fired. Cannon had been set within hearing distance all the way to the sea along the line of the canal. This way of sending news was the nearest approach to the telegraph at that time. Soon the tidings of the great event came booming down among the cliffs of the Hudson and reached New York.[1]

[1] The time allowed for the signaling from Buffalo to Sandy Hook was one hour and twenty minutes. This programme was substantially carried out. From Albany to Sandy Hook only twenty minutes were required.

THE ERIE CANAL

Two kegs of lake Erie water were put on one of the boats at Buffalo, and we shall see what was done with them. There were also two barrels of fine apples which had been raised in an orchard at Niagara Falls. These were not to be eaten on the way, one barrel being for the Town Council of Troy, and the other for the city fathers of New York. Many people on both sides of the ocean are still eating fine apples from the trees of the Genesee country.

One boat in the little fleet was called *Noah's Ark*, and on board were two eagles, a bear, some fawns, fishes, and birds, besides two Indian boys. These were sent to New York as "products of the West." At every town there was a celebration, and great was the excitement in such cities as Rochester, Syracuse, Utica, and Albany. There were salutes and feasts and speeches and prayers, and the gratitude and joy of the people fairly ran over. The greatest celebration of all was in New York, where everybody turned out to do honor to the occasion. The fine ladies boarded a special boat, and the "aquatic procession" went down through the bay to Sandy Hook. It was arranged that a messenger of Neptune, the sea god, should meet the fleet, inquire their errand, and lead them to his master's realm. Here Governor Clinton turned out the lake Erie water from the two kegs into the sea as a symbol of the joining of the lakes and the ocean. Then all the people went back to the city and had speeches and parades, feasts and fireworks, while the city-hall bell was rung for several hours. The illumination was said to be a fine one, but perhaps their lamps and candles would now look dim.

50 FROM TRAIL TO RAILWAY

After the canal was finished the carrying business was quite made over. Little was heard then about sending western New York fruit and grain to Philadelphia or Montreal or Alexandria. Freighting was so cheap that a man who had been selling his wheat for thirty cents a bushel now received a dollar for it. In the war with England, only a few years before, it had cost more to carry a cannon from Albany to Oswego than it had cost to make it. The journey had now become an easy and

FIG. 16. TRAVELING BY PACKET ON THE ERIE CANAL

simple matter. Two farmers built a boat of their own, loaded it with the produce of their farms, and took it down Seneca lake and all the way to New York. They were let out of the woods into the wide world.

The canal was not entirely given up to the carrying of freight. People thought that it was a fine experience to travel in the passenger boats, which were called "packets." These were considered as remarkable as are the limited express trains of to-day. The speed allowed by law was five miles an hour. To go faster would drive the water against the banks and injure them. The fare was five cents a mile including berth and table. It was said that a man could travel from New York to Buffalo with "the utmost comfort" and without fatigue. The journey cost eighteen dollars, and only took six days! We, of course, cannot help thinking of the Empire State Express, which leaves New York at 8.30 A.M. and arrives in Buffalo at 4.50 P.M.

FIG. 17. ERIE CANAL AND SOLVAY WORKS, SYRACUSE

If the journey of those days seems long to us, we must remember that to most of the travelers the scenery was fresh and interesting, for it was a visit to a new land. The rocky highlands, the blue Catskills, the winding Mohawk, and the towns and farms of the interior were perhaps as full of interest as the morning paper is on the trains of to-day. From Utica to Syracuse, more than fifty miles, is one great level; but on nearing Rochester the canal follows an embankment across a valley, and the passengers in those days looked wonderingly down on the tops of trees. At Lockport they heard the clatter as they slowly rose by a long row of locks to the top of the cliffs, and at Buffalo they looked out on a sea of fresh water. At Utica, Rome, Rochester, and other places, after a few years, side canals came in from north and south, from Binghamton and from the upper valley of the Genesee; and up in the hills great reservoirs were built, with shallow canals known as "feeders" leading down to the main trench These were built to make sure that there should be water enough for dry seasons; for locks will leak, and whenever a boat locks down a lockful of water goes on toward the sea.

Now all was stir and growth. Buffalo had started on its way to become a great city. Rochester ground more wheat and Syracuse made more salt. There was no doubt that New York would soon be known as the metropolis of the western world, and "Clinton's Ditch" became the most famous of American canals.

CHAPTER V

THE NEW YORK CENTRAL RAILWAY

The Erie canal had not long been finished when a new way of carrying men and merchandise came into use in New York. In the next year after the great celebration the legislature granted a charter to build a railroad from Albany to Schenectady. It is sometimes said that this was the first time in America that cars were drawn by means of steam. This is not true, but New York was not far behind some other states, and the De Witt Clinton train, of which a picture is shown in this chapter, looks as if it must have been one of the very earliest ones. This train made its trial trip in 1831, which was seventeen years after George Stephenson had built his first locomotive in England.

A railroad had been opened from Baltimore, a few miles to the west, the year before, and about the same time another was built in South Carolina. Two years earlier, in 1829, the Delaware and Hudson Canal Company brought from England three locomotives, one of them built by Stephenson, to draw coal to their canal from their mines at Honesdale, Pennsylvania. In 1826 a railroad four miles long was built at Quincy, Massachusetts, to carry granite from the quarries to the sea. It was called a tramway, and horses were used instead of steam. If we go to England, we shall find that tramways have been used there for more than a hundred years. Thus it is not easy to say when the first railroad was built, and all writers do not tell the same story about it, but it is certain that steam cars were first used and long roads with iron tracks were first built a little less than a hundred years ago.

If we study the De Witt Clinton train, we shall learn several things. Both the engine and the coaches were

FIG. 18. THE DE WITT CLINTON TRAIN

small and light compared with those used now. With the great speed of to-day, all the parts of a train must be very heavy in order to cling to the track. The engine of those days had four light driving wheels, and the engineer, it would seem, had to operate his engine while facing wind and storm. The cab looks very much like a common express wagon made heavier than usual; and if we look at the passenger wagons, we shall see why passenger cars are called coaches. The first ones *were* coaches.

and every picture of an old passenger train shows that the cars were modeled after the coaches of the stage lines of that age, except that the wheels were made with flat rims, with flanges to keep them on the track. The passengers certainly could not move about, and the high perches on the top look somewhat dangerous. One would think that the wind and the smoke of the locomotive could not have been pleasant. The men could not go into a smoking car, and if they had luncheon they must have brought it in their pockets. Nor could they tuck themselves snugly into a berth and sleep all night. These things, however, were not needed upon a railroad that was only eighteen miles long. To this day dining cars and "sleepers" are not so much used in England as in this country. Millions of people travel there, but the land is small, they go swiftly, and can usually eat and sleep at their journey's end. They still speak of the "wagons" of the "goods train," and English freight cars look almost like toys by the side of ours in America. This shows us how closely the railways and cars are related to common roads and vehicles.

People laughed at railroads in these early days and had about as much faith in them as we now have in flying machines. A few years ago men would have had the same sport about wireless telegraphy, or about talking between New York and Chicago with a telephone. Mrs. Alice Morse Earle, who has written much about early life in New England, says that the farmers did not like railroads, for they thought that horses would soon be useless and would then be killed, and that there would be no demand for oats or hay. They were afraid, too, that the noise would frighten the hens so that they would not lay, that the sparks from the engine would burn up everything, and that the people would go crazy.

There was some excuse for not enjoying railway travel, for the roadbeds were often made of solid rock, and the cars did not always have springs. The tracks were made of strap iron spiked down to wooden stringers. These iron straps would sometimes become loose, and had an unpleasant way of curling up and piercing the floor of the coach where people were sitting.

In these days it is more comfortable and probably safer to ride in a railway train than behind a horse. The Empire State Express runs from New York to Buffalo in eight hours and twenty minutes. It makes but four stops on the way and covers more than fifty-three miles an hour. When we compare this with the packet-boat time-table of seventy-five years ago we see how much time is now saved.

To-day a man can board the Twentieth Century Limited in New York City at 2.45 in the afternoon and be set down in Chicago the next morning. He can do business nearly all of one day by the sea, and nearly all of the next day on the shore of lake Michigan. On the way he will find easy chairs, books and papers, a good bed, a fine table, a place to write, to be shaved, or to take a bath, and he may even read from time to time the prices of stocks as they are sent over the wire from New York and Chicago. But our comfortable traveler should not despise the early days. Perhaps he misses some of the good times that the great-grandfathers had in the Mohawk boats and along the Genesee road.

THE NEW YORK CENTRAL RAILWAY 57

To go so fast and so far means that much has been done since the first small train came across the sand fields to Schenectady. Five years later the trains ran up to Utica. This was two hundred and two years after Arent Van Curler's journey along the same river. In two years more a little road, twenty-five miles long, had been finished between Syracuse and Auburn; but it was not until 1839, when another winter had passed, that the link between Utica and Syracuse was completed. This

Fig. 19. The Twentieth Century Limited

ran much of the way through woods and swamps, and in some cases timbers or piles had to be driven deep to hold up the track.

These roads were built by different companies, with no idea of joining them all into a through line. When, in time, there was talk of this the Utica people did not like it. They thought that it would ruin the business of their town if passengers and freight need not be changed there and if trains went rushing through. But after a while all the links between New York and Buffalo were forged into one chain, or became a "trunk line," to put it in the modern way. Of course it would cost less to haul

Genesee flour or Niagara county apples to New York if they could go through in the same car in which they were first locked. This soon became so plain that there was no further question as to uniting the various roads. We shall see how they all became one.

Cornelius Vanderbilt was of Dutch descent and was born on Staten island in 1794. He grew up in the steamboat business, and by industry and foresight became the owner of various lines plying on the Hudson, along the coast, and even across the Atlantic. He had so much to do with shipping that at length he was known as "Commodore" Vanderbilt, although this was a nickname and not a real title. By and by he began to buy railroads, and by 1869 he was able to unite those of the Hudson and those west of Albany into the New York Central and Hudson River Railroad. His descendants have bought or leased many other roads, which, taken together, are often called the Vanderbilt system. This reaches far westward into many states and joins other great cities to the metropolis by lines of steel.

Railways in Michigan and Ohio were tied to Vanderbilt's road, and wheat and many other products came to Buffalo not only on cars but by ships on the Great Lakes, and were then sent to New York and across the ocean. So the canal gradually did less business and the railroad did more, for people could travel faster by rail, and some things, like meat and fruit, must be carried swiftly or they will spoil on the way. Now, instead of ten-ton boats on the Mohawk, or the slow-going craft of "Clinton's Ditch," great freight trains rush down

THE NEW YORK CENTRAL RAILWAY 59

the Mohawk valley, bearing nearly a hundred thousand bushels of grain behind one engine. Such a load would have fed George Washington's armies for a long time. After a while one track was not sufficient for so many trains going east and west. Too much time was lost in waiting on sidings and there was danger of collision. For this reason a second track was put down, then a

FIG. 20. ROUNDING THE NOSES, MOHAWK VALLEY

third and a fourth, and now all the way from Albany to Buffalo there are two tracks for passenger trains and two for freight. Down the Hudson there are but two tracks, because the space between the river and the uplands is so narrow. Many years ago a rival road, called the West Shore Railway, was built along the west bank of the Hudson, and then westward to Buffalo. This with its two tracks was bought by the owners of the Central road, so that now they have six tracks across the state. Even these are hardly enough, for every year the great West has more people, raises more grain to ship to eastern cities and to Europe, and requires more goods from mills and factories along the Atlantic coast.

There are many local trains that run between New York and Albany, or Albany and Syracuse, or Syracuse and Buffalo. These are convenient for the smaller towns and cities. Then there are many through trains whose destination is Buffalo, Detroit, Chicago, Indianapolis, or St. Louis. Quickly changing cars at lake Michigan or the Mississippi river, the traveler is hurried on to the Rocky mountains, the Pacific ocean, Alaska, or the lands of Asia or Australia across the sea.

The New York Central is not the only great road that runs westward through the state. The Erie road was built through the southern counties from New York to lake Erie, partly because the townships through which it runs were jealous of the privileges which the great canal gave to the people farther north. The Delaware, Lackawanna and Western also comes from New York through the coal region of Pennsylvania, and runs near the Erie road to Buffalo.

The larger cities and the greater number of towns are, however, along the Central Railway. Going up the Hudson and the Mohawk, the traveler will hardly pass one busy town before he is in sight of another. When he looks across the river and sees Newburg he will remember that in a plain old house in that city General Washington had his headquarters. When he comes in sight of Albany he will see the great Capitol building

THE NEW YORK CENTRAL RAILWAY   61

standing high over all others. At Schenectady he will think of Arent Van Curler and the old boatmen and the dreadful French and Indian massacre. At Utica he will pass the ford where thousands waded the river as they went to the wilderness. At Rome he will be reminded of the famous carry of Fort Stanwix, of St. Leger, and of the heroes who drove him back to the north. At Syracuse he will ride through miles of closely built streets, and as he leaves the city on the west he will see ancient vats with low sliding roofs. In these vats countless bushels of salt have been made, as the sun has slowly drawn off the water of the brine in vapor. There were buildings, too, with chimneys and great boilers for making salt; but in the main the city has other interests now. It has mills and large stores, and is a railway center.

At Rochester our traveler crosses the Genesee, and remembers the hardy pioneer who left comfortable old Hagerstown to build a city in the swamp and forest. Colonel Rochester could have had no idea of the fine city he was starting, or of the orchards, nurseries, and wheat fields that would be around it, but he lived long enough to see the flour mills at the falls doing a thriving business. Thus wheat and flour made Rochester as salt made Syracuse, and first the canal and then the great railway took these useful things to market.

An hour or two more and the train pulls into Buffalo, the second city of New York, looking on the lake and stretching out its hands to the great world of inland sea and prairie. To Buffalo come coal and iron and meat and wheat and corn. Here great elevators receive grain from the ships and load canal boats and railway cars for the east. Here some of the New York Central trains turn north and go by Niagara through Canada to the west, while others pass off to the south and west and go to Cleveland, Toledo, and Chicago. Since the day when the two kegs were filled with water from lake Erie, Buffalo has become a large city, a gateway of the East and West. And since the De Witt Clinton train crept from Albany to Schenectady, the New York Central Railway has become great also, for every day hundreds of trains of goods and men are coming and going between the Lakes and the city by the sea.

CHAPTER VI

OLD JOURNEYS FROM PHILADELPHIA TO THE WEST

The people of New York City like to say that Philadelphia is slow, and would almost make one think that all the men there wear Quaker hats and act like William Penn. The citizens of Philadelphia, however, are not much troubled by this, for they have a great and busy city, and they like to remind the men of New York that Philadelphia is a "city of homes," and that the people do not live in great tenement houses nor do all their business in "sky scrapers." The Liberty Bell hangs there, the Continental Congress sat there, and the home of the federal government was there before it was in Washington. For a long time the Quaker City was the metropolis of America, but as New York and Baltimore grew they took away some of the trade that otherwise would have gone to the city on the Delaware. It also ceased to be the capital of the nation and thus had to depend more on its shipping and inland business. Now to do much inland business it was necessary not only to reach the rich lowlands at hand but also to send out across the mountains. This could not be done without roads.

When men went from New York City across the mountains they found the Great Lakes and the rich plains on their shores. So Philadelphia, looking over her mountain wall, saw the noble valley of the Ohio river and the young Pittsburg at its gateway. As New York found a route to the West, so Philadelphia sought out its highways to the country beyond the Appalachian mountains. In this chapter and the next we shall see where these highways ran.

The first roads were little like those of to-day, and the stage drivers had to be steady, cool-headed men. There were many stumps and logs in what was called a road, and the teams were guided less by reins than by shouts in a kind of language which the horses understood. A traveler between Philadelphia and Washington said that often the driver would call to the passengers to lean out of the carriage on one side or the other, so that their weight might keep the balance even. He would say, "Now, gentlemen, to the right!" and the men would lean out as far as they could; or, "Now, gentlemen, to the left!" and over they would swing to the other side.

It took strong wagons to travel such roads, and sometimes the wheels were cut solid by sawing off short sections of the butt of a great tree, much as the wheels of a toy cart have been made by many boys. When a driver was stuck in the mud he had to wait for other teams to come up, when they would hook on with him and drag him out upon hard ground again. They were a rough but sociable company, the teamsters of those days, feeding their horses and cracking their jokes at the taverns which lined the turnpikes. They would stand by one another loyally, but when they met some

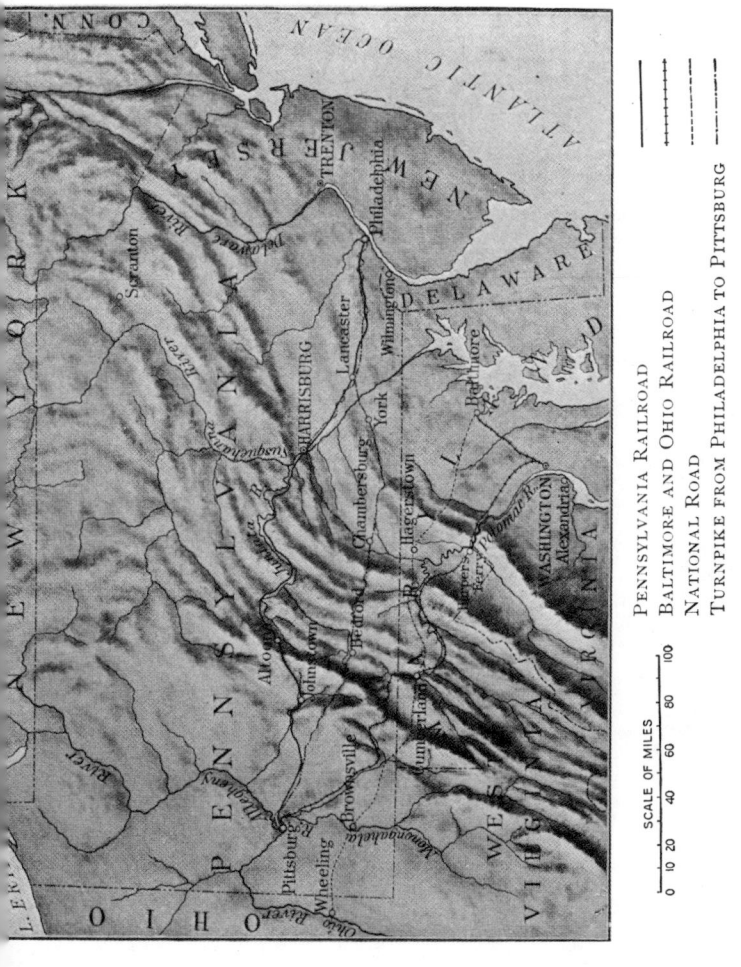

PENNSYLVANIA RAILROAD
BALTIMORE AND OHIO RAILROAD
NATIONAL ROAD
TURNPIKE FROM PHILADELPHIA TO PITTSBURG

OLD JOURNEYS FROM PHILADELPHIA 65

fine gentleman on the road they did not object to taking off a wheel or crushing the frame of his light carriage.

Out of West Philadelphia to-day leads a street known as Lancaster avenue. It is the eastern end of the old "Lancaster pike," the town which gave name to the road being sixty-six miles to the west. This is the oldest turnpike road in the United States. When the pioneers

FIG. 21. PENN SQUARE, LANCASTER, PENNSYLVANIA, LOOKING EAST ALONG THE "LANCASTER PIKE"

were clearing up the forests and building the Genesee road in New York this region was already well settled. If you ride from Philadelphia to Lancaster to-day, you will see that it is an old country, and you will not think it strange when you learn that so long ago as 1730, two years before the birth of Washington, some of the inhabitants were moving out beyond Lancaster. This means that they went west of the Susquehanna, for Lancaster is only about twelve miles east of that great river.

Many of the earlier settlers of this lowland region west of Philadelphia were Germans. William Penn had invited some of these people to come, and they had settled near by in the place now known as Germantown. In time many others settled both around Lancaster and farther west. Hence we hear of "Pennsylvania Dutch," although they were not really Dutch, which is a term belonging rather to Hollanders and their descendants. There were also some Scotch-Irish, as they were called, — descendants of Scotch people who had migrated to the north of Ireland, whence their children had come to America. These were Presbyterians, and some of them had settled in New Jersey, where they founded Princeton College.

The country between Philadelphia and the Susquehanna is one of the richest and most fertile regions in the world. Most of it is low, with gently rolling fields and a few higher hills. One fine farm joins another, and the great stone houses look as strong and as solid as if they had grown up out of the ground. Huge chimneys rise from the roofs and make one think of the warm fire-places and well-spread tables of the thrifty German farmers who built these houses and lived in them. The barns, like the houses, are large; they are often built of stone and whitewashed, and they still hold great harvests. One side of the barn usually reaches several feet beyond the high foundation, and is called an "overshoot." As the doors to the stables are under this, it seems to have been planned as a protection against storms.

OLD JOURNEYS FROM PHILADELPHIA 67

An English traveler went over the Lancaster pike in 1796 and found it worthy of praise. He said that it was paved with stone, covered with gravel, and could be traversed in any season of the year. About one mile east of the public square in Lancaster a fine old arched bridge of stone carries the turnpike across Conestoga creek, a stream flowing southward into the Susquehanna.

FIG. 22. BRIDGE ON THE "PIKE" CROSSING CONESTOGA CREEK ONE MILE EAST OF PENN SQUARE, LANCASTER, PENNSYLVANIA

It takes its name, which has become famous in American history, from a small tribe of Indians who lived on its borders. The early inhabitants made the water deeper by building dams with locks, and sailed their boats with loads of produce down to the Susquehanna. In the common phrase of that time, they spoke of it as the "Conestoga navigation."

But the most interesting thing to which the name Conestoga was given was a wagon that was invented in this region. It was made very large and strong, to carry freight, and was drawn by four, seven, or even a dozen horses. Hundreds of these wagons were to be seen on the Lancaster pike and on the other great roads of that time. They were built, as freight cars are now, to carry heavy loads long distances in safety.

These wagons were unusually long, and the boxes curved upward at the ends, so that inside and out they

FIG. 23. TOLLHOUSE EIGHT MILES EAST OF LANCASTER, PENNSYLVANIA

were shaped somewhat like a canoe. The advantage of this was that the loads did not slide, but rode steadily when the wagons went up and down steep hills. The wheels were big and had wide tires, so that the heavy loads would not cut the roads. The story is told that one of these wagons with its load of tobacco weighed more than thirteen thousand pounds, or almost seven tons.

They were painted red and blue, and were covered with a canopy of cloth, so that they looked like the "prairie schooners" which in later days were the emigrant wagons of the western plains. Each wagon had a tool box fastened at the side, and a tar bucket and a water pail hung beneath. The horses were well fed, well matched, and strong, with good harnesses and many jingling bells. The drivers were rough-and-ready men, who snapped their whips in the daytime, told stories in the evening, and slept at night on little mattresses of their own in front of the barroom fire.

Hundreds of these wagons were going and coming on the roads in the days when people were not dreaming of freight trains, and no doubt the Conestoga seemed as important then as the chief freight lines now appear to us. In the French and Indian War, when there was great need of wagons to carry Braddock's stores, Benjamin Franklin was asked to get some of these famous conveyances. He succeeded, for many were to be found in this part of Pennsylvania, and he sent on more than one hundred and fifty of them. He nearly lost his fortune in consequence, for he told the farmers he would see that they were paid if the wagons and horses were not returned. It cost the old patriot twenty thousand pounds, but fortunately the government afterwards paid the money back to him. Not long ago the writer saw one of these wagons, with a boat-shaped box, but without a canopy, in use on a farm near Lancaster.

Following the pike westward for twelve miles from Lancaster, the traveler crosses the Susquehanna river at Columbia. The old bridge was destroyed long ago, but the present one, although it looks new, is hardly used in a modern way. It is narrow, with a plank floor, and it serves for railway trains and wagons, as well as for foot passengers. There is no separate place for any of these, so when a train or wagon goes on at either end a telegram is sent to the other end to keep cars and carriages from entering the bridge there.

FIG. 24. HAMBRIGHT'S HOTEL, ON THE "PIKE," THREE MILES WEST OF LANCASTER, PENNSYLVANIA

Along the "Pike" is an electric road, which carries people more swiftly and doubtless with less dust and jolting than did the old stages. Hambright's Hotel, shown in the picture above, is on this road, and, with its big chimneys and high, long-handled pump, shows how many of the ancient hotels looked. They seem lonely enough now, but they were gay and busy places then. It is very appropriate that the company which runs all the street cars in and about Lancaster calls itself The Conestoga Traction Company.

OLD JOURNEYS FROM PHILADELPHIA 71

Westward from the Susquehanna, in what we shall know in a later chapter as the Great Valley, are some comfortable old towns bearing the names of Carlisle, Shippensburg, and Chambersburg. The pike passes through these and on to the old town of Bedford. Then it enters a high, rough strip of land that was covered with forest long after Philadelphia had become a city

FIG. 25. OLD ROAD HOUSE, ONE MILE WEST OF CHAMBERSBURG, PENNSYLVANIA

and the farmers about Lancaster had built their great houses and barns. At the other end of this wilderness was Pittsburg. The road from Bedford to Pittsburg was cut through the woods in 1758, in the time of the French and Indian wars, and is sometimes called Forbes's road, from the general who directed the making of it. It was used in the time of the Revolution, and many forts were built to guard it.

This roadway was so important that the Pennsylvania government, a few years after the Revolutionary War, took it in hand and improved it. Thus there was a line of travel over the older highway to Lancaster and Bedford, and thence over the newer road to Pittsburg. The whole road led from the seaboard to the Ohio river and was often called the Pittsburg pike.

We have now learned of two great, well-trodden routes from east to west, — the route of the Hudson and the Mohawk through New York, and the route through the southern parts of Pennsylvania from Philadelphia to Pittsburg.

In laying out such roads the pioneers almost always followed trails that the Indians had made. For long generations the red men had followed the same paths, beating them smooth and deep in the forest earth. The white men widened the trail by using pack horses, loading the beasts well with all sorts of things. The next step was to cut away trees, take out the stones, and make roads for wagons. Carrying by pack horses, however, had become a great business, and the horse owners were very angry when the wagons began to take away their trade.

In 1830 a Pennsylvania citizen, then nearly a hundred years old, told of seeing the first wagon reach Carlisle, and he remembered how furious the "packers" were because they feared that they would lose their business. It did not occur to them that they could harness their horses into teams, buy strong wagons, and be ready to make money in the new way instead of the old. The horse owners were quite as angry about stagecoaches, and they sometimes destroyed the coaches and injured the passengers to vent their spite. Moreover, as people often like an excuse for doing wrong, and for harboring mean feelings, these men said that the stage business was bad for the cloth makers and tailors, because people could ride in coaches without spoiling their fine clothes, whereas when they rode on horseback they soon ruined them and had to buy new ones. Almost any excuse will serve those to whom no way seems good except their own.

Philadelphia now had its connection with Pittsburg and the Ohio river and the rich lands bordering it, as New York had its way leading to Buffalo and the Great Lakes and the prairies. But the southern road crossed a rougher country than did the northern one, and so it was less easily kept in order and was harder to travel. Hence Philadelphia, like New York, sought better means of communication with the country on the other side of the mountains.

CHAPTER VII

THE PENNSYLVANIA RAILROAD

A horse railroad had been built from Philadelphia to the Susquehanna river, and the big Conestoga wagons were running along the pike to Pittsburg; but this was not enough. New York had stirred the whole country by its great canal, and the people along the Potomac were thinking of similar schemes. Pennsylvania could not rest idle, and decided to have a canal of its own.

In 1826 the ditch was begun at Columbia, where the railroad ended, and, following the custom of the times, those in charge started the work on Independence Day. In four years they had dug the canal, let in the water, and were running boats as far as Harrisburg.

A few miles above Harrisburg the canal turned away from the main river and followed its great western branch, the Juniata. This river cuts through the high ridges, or flows between them as best it can, taking a very winding course. The valley is often narrow and its sides are steep and rugged. Still it has no heavy grades along the bottom, and it led the canal diggers far into the mountains, to a village called Hollidaysburg.

Here the highlands are so steep that the canal had to stop. The Allegheny Front is almost fourteen hundred feet above Hollidaysburg, and on the other side the

THE PENNSYLVANIA RAILROAD

Conemaugh river rushes swiftly down past the city of Johnstown, which is seven hundred and seventy-one feet below the summit. Hollidaysburg and Johnstown are thirty-eight miles apart, and the uplands lying between are so steep and high that to cut through them was out of the question. But those who were interested in the canal were not to be beaten, and they kept on digging both to the east and to the west. Beyond Johnstown they carried the canal to the Ohio river at Pittsburg.

Meantime the high grounds on the divide were not neglected. A famous road, the Allegheny Portage Railway, was built with several inclined planes. Stationary engines pulled the cars up each slope, but on the level parts of the road they were drawn by horses.

FIG. 26. FREIGHT LOCOMOTIVE, PENNSYLVANIA RAILROAD

76   FROM TRAIL TO RAILWAY

The road was not carried to the top, but nearly two hundred feet below a tunnel was cut about a mile long. The entrance to one end of this tunnel is shown in Fig. 27.

The two great sections of the canal and the Portage Railway were finished in 1835. Goods then went by

FIG. 27. ENTRANCE TO TUNNEL, OLD PORTAGE RAILWAY

rail from Philadelphia to Columbia on the Susquehanna river. There the boats took them to the east end of the Portage road. The next haul was over the Allegheny Front, with its lofty forests, to Johnstown. Then the boats received the merchandise and landed it in Pittsburg, whence other boats could carry it to any town on the Ohio river.

THE PENNSYLVANIA RAILROAD 77

The *Hit or Miss* was one of the boats that came up to Hollidaysburg. It was desirable to take this particular boat over the heights, so a car was built which would fit its keel. The car was dragged up the east side of the mountain and down to Johnstown, where the boat

FIG. 28. BROAD STREET STATION, PHILADELPHIA: PENNSYLVANIA RAILROAD

was put into the water again and sent off to the Mississippi river. We can now look across a gorge from the coaches of the Pennsylvania Railroad, beyond Altoona, and see the grade of the old Portage Railway.

The canal almost put out of business the Conestoga wagons on the dusty pike which had seen so much travel by way of Carlisle and Bedford. But the people did not stop with a canal. Like the men of New York, they wanted something even better than that. They wished to have a railroad all the way, and in 1846 the Pennsylvania Railroad Company was incorporated. By this time it was very well known that railroads were successful both in America and in England, and that steam was better than horses.

Over the Allegheny Front a route was found where the grades were not too steep for locomotives. The grade, of course, had been the one great hindrance to the whole project, and when this difficulty was overcome there was no reason why passengers should not be carried from Philadelphia to Pittsburg, or a load of iron from Pittsburg to Philadelphia, without changing cars. In the year 1854 the Pennsylvania people triumphed, for they had conquered the mountains and could run trains from the banks of the Delaware to the Ohio river.

If we leave Philadelphia by the great Broad street station of the Pennsylvania Railroad, we shall pass out among the pleasant homes of West Philadelphia and through the fine farms of the Pennsylvania lowlands, until we come, in about an hour and a half, to the staid old city of Lancaster. We have been here before, to learn of turnpikes and Conestoga freighters

The next stop, if we are on an express train, will be at Harrisburg, a little more than a hundred miles from Philadelphia. We have now come from the Delaware to the Susquehanna, and are close to the mountains. Before we go in among them let us see Harrisburg. It is a city of fifty thousand people, and lies along the east bank of the Susquehanna, which here is a great river a mile wide, having gathered its tribute of waters from hundreds of branching streams in Pennsylvania and New York.

Not far to the east a small stream runs parallel to the main river, and the larger part of Harrisburg is on higher ground between the two. On the highest part of this ridge is the state capitol, a great building but recently finished. Harrisburg is at the right point for the state government. It is not in the center of the state, to be sure, but it is at the rear of the lowlands which

FIG. 29. BRIDGE, PENNSYLVANIA RAILROAD, ABOVE HARRISBURG

reach in from the sea, and is just outside the great gateway where roads from all the northern, western, and central uplands come out on the plain. It is a convenient center for coal and iron, and hence one sees along the river below the city many blast furnaces, rolling mills, and factories. To the northeast rich, open lands stretch along the base of Blue mountain, and railroads join Harrisburg to Reading, Allentown, Bethlehem, and Easton. To the southwest bridges cross the Susquehanna, and roads run to Carlisle, Hagerstown, and other cities of the Great Valley (Chapter XI).

Thus the Pennsylvania Railroad, running northwest from Philadelphia, crosses at Harrisburg other roads that run to the southwest. As hamlets often gather about "four corners" in the country, so cities grow up where the great roads of the world cross each other.

FIG. 30. PENNSYLVANIA RAILROAD SHOPS, ALTOONA

Leaving Harrisburg behind, we pass the splendid new bridge of the Pennsylvania Railroad, across the Susquehanna (Fig. 29), and go through the gap in Blue mountain. Soon we turn away from the main river and enter the winding valley of the Juniata. The grades are easy, the roadbed is smooth, and by deep cuts through the rocks the curves have been made less abrupt. It is only when one looks out of the car window that the land is found to be rugged and mountainous.

All the greater valleys and ridges of the mountain belt of Pennsylvania run northeast and southwest. The last of these to be crossed on our journey is Bald Eagle valley, from which the Allegheny Front rises to the northwest.

In this valley, near the place where the Portage Railway began to scale the heights, and a little more than a

THE PENNSYLVANIA RAILROAD

hundred miles from Pittsburg, the Pennsylvania Railroad Company in 1850 founded a town and called it Altoona. Here they started shops, which have now grown to notable importance. The town became a city eighteen years after it was begun, and has to-day about forty thousand inhabitants. In the railway shops alone may be found nine thousand men repairing and building locomotives, passenger coaches, and freight cars. The Pennsylvania Railroad Company is now founding a great school in Altoona, where young men may be taught to become skillful and efficient in railway service.

FIG. 31. HORSESHOE CURVE, PENNSYLVANIA RAILROAD

Altoona looks new, and with its endless freight yards, its noisy shops, and its sooty cover of smoke from burning soft coal, it is very different from quiet Lancaster, which was old when forests covered the site of Altoona.

On our way to Pittsburg we are soon pulling up the Allegheny Front by a great loop, or bend, which enables the tracks to reach the summit more than a thousand feet above Altoona. Nestling within the great bend is a reservoir of water to supply the houses and shops of the city lying below. Passing the highest point, we find ourselves descending the valley of the Conemaugh river to Johnstown, and surrounded by the high lands of the Allegheny plateau.

Johnstown is much older than Altoona, for it was settled in 1791, but it has not grown so fast, and has only about as many inhabitants as the city of railroad shops. Most people know of Johnstown because of the flood which ruined the place in 1889. Several miles above the town was a reservoir more than two miles long and in several places one hundred feet deep. After the heavy rains of that spring the dam broke on the last day of May, and the wild rush of waters destroyed the town. Homes, stores, shops, and mills were torn away and carried down the river. Clara Barton of the Red Cross, who went to Johnstown as soon as she could get there, says that the few houses that were not crushed and strewn along the valley were turned upside down.

More than two thousand men, women, and children lost their lives, and those that were left were in mourning and poverty. The whole land sent in its gifts of money, clothing, and food, and the town was built up again into a prosperous city. Near the city are found coal, iron, limestone, and fire clay, and these things make it easy to establish iron works. The Cambria Steel Company gives work to ten thousand men in its shops, mines, and furnaces.

The main line of the Pennsylvania Railroad runs down the rugged Conemaugh valley through Johnstown, and is its chief means of traffic. As we go on to the west we near Pittsburg, but first we pass through a number of stirring towns. At one place fire bricks are made, and the clay for molding them and the coal for burning them are found in the same hill. In another town there are coal mines and glass works. Farther west the Pennsylvania road has more repair shops, and Braddock is the great Carnegie town. We shall see why many thriving young cities have grown up in this region when we take up Pittsburg, about which they are all clustered.

At Pittsburg we pull into one of the finest railway stations in the United States. We may stop in the city of coal and iron, or we may go on to the west, over one of the main arms of the Pennsylvania Railroad system. If we take the northern branch, it will carry us across Ohio to Fort Wayne in Indiana and to Chicago. If we board a train on the southern arm, we shall go through Columbus and Indianapolis, and be set down on the farther side of the Mississippi river at St. Louis.

North and south from the great east and west trunk lines run many shorter roads, or "spurs." On the east there is a network of short roads in New Jersey, and one of the busiest parts of the whole system is that which joins Washington to Baltimore, Philadelphia, and New York.

West from Philadelphia for a long distance there are four tracks, and on either side may be seen neat hedges, such as one finds along the railways of England. In the mountains it is often hard to make a roadbed wide enough for four tracks, and hence there may be only

Fig. 32. Rock Cut, along the Line of the Pennsylvania Railroad

three or even two in some places. No doubt four will in time be built through to Pittsburg, for many millions of dollars are spent in improving the road. Instead of having a long circuit around the hills, tunnels and vast cuts in the bed rock are made so as to straighten the line. Thus both passenger and freight trains are able to

THE PENNSYLVANIA RAILROAD 85

make better time, and the road can carry the stores of iron and coal which are found in the lands on either side.

Some of the freight yards are always crowded with cars, and at Harrisburg the company is building separate tracks around the city, so that through freight trains need not be delayed.

At New York the Pennsylvania Railroad now has its station on the New Jersey side of the Hudson river, but it is building a tunnel under the river. The company has already bought several city blocks and has torn away the buildings. Here it will build one of the greatest passenger stations in the world. The tunnel will run on to the east, under the streets and shops of Manhattan, and under the East river. Thus under New York and its surrounding waters trains can go to the east end of Long Island.

Pennsylvania has told us the same story that we learned from New York. We read it again: first, how the Indian's path was beaten deeper and wider by the hoofs of the pack horse, bearing goods to sell and barter in the wilderness; then how strips of forest were cut down to make room for the Conestoga wagons and the gay stages that swept through from Philadelphia to Pittsburg. These in their turn became old-fashioned when the canal and Portage Railway were done, and now we sit in a car that is like a palace, and think canals and Conestogas very old stories indeed. In future generations swift air ships may take the wonder away from the Empire State Express, and make us listen unmoved when a man, standing in the station at Philadelphia, calls the limited train for Pittsburg, Cincinnati, and St. Louis.

CHAPTER VIII

THE NATIONAL ROAD

The sea reaches inland almost to the northeast corner of the state of Maryland. This long, wide arm of the ocean receives many rivers and is known as Chesapeake bay. Near its north end is Baltimore, one of the four great cities of our Atlantic coast. It is one hundred and fifty miles from the open sea. If, instead of sailing up the bay, we should turn toward the west, we could go up the Potomac river, which is deep and wide. On our way we should pass Washington's estates at Mount Vernon, the old city of Alexandria, and the national capital, Washington. We could not sail much farther because there are falls in the Potomac which ships cannot pass. The Potomac runs so close to Chesapeake bay that it is only forty miles from Washington across to Baltimore.

Chesapeake bay is much like Delaware bay and the tidal Hudson river, only it is larger than either. Baltimore is at a greater distance from the open sea than Philadelphia is, and Philadelphia is farther inland than New York, but each of these cities tried to get as much of the western trade as it could.

The natural way for the men of Baltimore and Alexandria to go across to the west was up the Potomac river and through its passes in the mountains. But before they tried this they had settled much of the low, flat land along the Potomac and about the Chesapeake in Virginia and Maryland. This was often called "tidewater country," because the beds of the rivers are below sea level, and the streams are deep enough for boats of some size.

When the land was first settled and the colonists found that they could go almost everywhere by boat,

FIG. 33. TOLLHOUSE WEST OF BROWNSVILLE, PENNSYLVANIA

they paid small heed to making roads. They could visit their neighbors on other plantations and they could load their tobacco and take it to market by the rivers. Many plantations were beside rivers of such great depth that sailing vessels bound for London could come up to the farmer's wharf and get his crop of tobacco.

In early days the members of the legislature were not always given so much per mile to pay the stage fares between their homes and the capital, but they were allowed the cost of hiring boats instead. Many ferries were needed, and laws about them were made before rules were laid down for bridges and roads. Several lawmakers at one time would have been fined for their absence from the legislature of the colony had they not been excused because there was no ferry to carry them over the river which they would have had to cross.

Around Annapolis "rolling roads" were made. These were wide paths made as smooth as possible, in order that large hogsheads of tobacco might be rolled, each by two men, to the market in that old town.

After a time the lowlands of the coast region began to fill up and the people were pushing westward, just as they did in Pennsylvania and New York. No man had so great a part in this westward movement as the young surveyor, George Washington. In 1748 he was sixteen years old, a tall, strong lad, full of courage and energy. Lord William Fairfax, a rich English gentleman who had settled in Virginia, had bought great tracts of forest land up the Potomac behind the Blue Ridge mountains, and he was eager to have them surveyed. Knowing that Washington had studied surveying, Fairfax asked him to undertake the task. The boy consented; he went beyond the Blue Ridge into the country along the Shenandoah, camped in the woods, swam the rivers, toughened his muscles, learned the ways of the red men, and three years later came back, a grown man, ready for great things.

While Washington was getting his practice as a surveyor the Ohio Company was formed to take up lands along the Ohio river, and to keep the French from settling there. Lawrence, Washington's elder brother, was one of the chief men of this company. In 1753 Washington himself went west to the Ohio river. Day by day the French were taking a firmer hold of that country, and Dinwiddie, the old Scottish governor of Virginia, looked about for some one to carry a warning letter to the commander of one of their new forts. The messenger was also to keep his eyes open and report what the French were doing on the upper waters of the Ohio. He chose Washington, saying, "Faith, you're a brave lad, and, if you play your cards well, you shall have no cause to repent your bargain." Washington did not wait, but left on the day he received his commission, late in October, 1753.

Christopher Gist, a famous frontiersman, was secured as guide, and we can have no doubt that he and Washington formed a team, ready to meet Frenchmen, red men, and the dangers of river and forest. They made up their little party where the city of Cumberland, Maryland, now stands. It is far up the Potomac, in the heart of the mountains, — a long way beyond the Blue Ridge and the lands where Washington had been surveying.

At this place a large stream called Wills creek cuts through one of the mountain ridges by a deep gorge and enters the Potomac. On a hill, where these streams come together, was Fort Cumberland, the great outpost of Virginia and Maryland. A fine church now stands on the ground of the old fort, in the heart of the busy city of Cumberland. This was the starting point for Washington's expedition and for many later ones into the western wilderness.

Washington made his dangerous journey with success. He brought back a letter from the French commander, but of much greater value was the story of all that he had seen. The colonists now knew just what they would have to do to keep possession of the Ohio lands.

It was not long before Washington went again as commanding officer of a small army, and in 1755 he served under General Braddock in the famous battle which resulted in the defeat of the English and the death of their general. Washington, as we know, brought off the troops with honor to himself. In each of these expeditions something was done toward cutting away the trees and grading a road from Fort Cumberland to the head of the Ohio river at Pittsburg.

FIG. 34. MILESTONE ON THE LINE OF BRADDOCK'S ROAD, NEAR FROSTBURG, MARYLAND

On the line of Braddock's road, a dozen miles west of Cumberland, is a milestone, set up about a hundred and fifty years ago. A photograph of it is shown above. It is a rough brown stone, standing in a pasture half a mile outside the city of Frostburg, in western Maryland. The stone was once taken away and broken, but it has since been set up again and cemented into a base of concrete. The view shows how it has been split up and down. On one side are directions, and on the other are the words, "Our Country's Rights We Will Defend."

Braddock's journey from Alexandria to Fort Duquesne was an uncomfortable one, to say nothing of its disastrous end. He bought a carriage to ride in, but the road was not suited to a coach, as were the roads he knew in old England. Beyond Cumberland, especially, in spite of all the work his men could do upon it, it was so bad that he was forced to take Washington's advice and change the baggage from wagons to pack horses.

Gradually, as time went on, these rough paths were beaten down into smoother thoroughfares. The same causes that led to the development of the North were working also at the South. Along the Potomac, as in New York and in Pennsylvania, the stream of colonial life flowed westward. First the pioneers settled the lowlands around Chesapeake bay and along the deep rivers; then as their strength and courage reached beyond the mountains they found the forests and fertile soil behind the Blue Ridge. Farther within the rugged highlands they built Fort Cumberland and sent out discoverers and armies to the Ohio river. When the woods were cleared and towns and states grew up on the Ohio, there was frequent occasion to cross the mountains for trade, for travel, and to reach the seat of government, which in 1801 was moved to Washington on the Potomac.

These glimpses of colonial journeys will help us to understand why the National Road came to be built. About one hundred years ago the government began to take a great interest in opening roads, especially across the Appalachian mountains, to Ohio, Kentucky, and other parts of the Mississippi valley. Washington, who died in 1799, had said much about this work, for he not only wanted western trade to come to Virginia instead of going to New Orleans, but he also felt that so long as the mountains kept the East and the West apart we should never have one common country, held together by friendly feelings.

FIG. 35. OLD ROAD HOUSE, BROWNSVILLE, PENNSYLVANIA

The people of Baltimore, like those of New York and Philadelphia, were eager to have the best road to the West, that their business might be benefited. Not far from Baltimore is an old place called Joppa, and several roads are still known as "Joppa roads." The town is older than Baltimore and was once the chief trading town in the northern part of Maryland; but Baltimore was well situated on an arm of the great bay, and by this time had gone far ahead of its old rival.

THE NATIONAL ROAD

A number of good roads had been built in Maryland, among them a famous one leading out westward to Frederick. This was in the direction of Hagerstown, and still farther west was Cumberland. The United States government decided to build a great road to Ohio, beginning at Cumberland. To get the benefit of this, the men of Baltimore went to work to push the Frederick pike westward to the beginning of the National Road.

So it came about in 1811 that the first contracts were let for building parts of the National Road. We remember that the Erie canal was not started until six years later. The act of Congress which ordered the making of the road provided that a strip four rods wide should be cleared of trees, that it should be built up in the middle with broken stone, gravel, or other material good for roads, and that all steep slopes should be avoided. The road was opened to the public in 1818, one year after the Erie canal was begun. The original plan was to make it seven hundred miles long, reaching from Cumberland to the Mississippi river, but it was never carried out.

The Maryland roads, as we have seen, ran west from Baltimore and Washington to Frederick, east of the Blue Ridge; to Hagerstown, in the Great Valley; and to Cumberland, in the mountains. Cumberland is a stirring town of about twenty thousand people, and with its great business in coal, iron, and railroads it seems like a larger city. Thence the National Road runs through the gap in Wills mountain (Fig. 36) to Frostburg, a dozen miles west and fifteen hundred feet higher. The road soon bears northward into Pennsylvania and crosses the Monongahela river at Brownsville, about forty miles south of Pittsburg. Coal is mined here, and boats were running in those early days, as coal barges and steamboats run to-day, down to the great iron city.

From Brownsville the pike leads over the hills and comes down to the Ohio river at Wheeling, West Virginia. It then passes on through Ohio, touching Columbus, the capital, on the way to Indiana and the Mississippi.

We sometimes admire the cars marked with the sign of the United States post office, which we see drawn by a swift locomotive at a speed of sixty miles an hour; but when the government put its mail coaches on the National Road from Washington to Wheeling, no doubt they seemed quite as wonderful to the people of that time. And it was only twenty-five years since the people of Utica had thought it so remarkable that six letters had come to them in one mail! Soon passenger coaches were rushing along at ten miles an hour, and sometimes even faster. There were canvas-covered freight wagons, each of which carried ten tons, had rear wheels ten feet high, and was drawn by twelve horses. In those days life was full of stirring interest on the National Road.

There were rates of toll for all sorts of animals and wagons. The toll was higher for hogs than for sheep, and more was charged for cattle than for hogs. If the wagons had very wide tires, no toll was demanded. Drivers sometimes lied about the number of people in their stages, so as to pay less toll. The stages were not owned by the drivers but by companies, which bid for travelers and freight, as railways do now. There were penalties for injuring milestones or defacing bridges, showing that some people then were like some people

Fig. 36. Cumberland and the Gap in Wills Mountain

now. The companies had interesting names. There were the "Good Intent," "Ohio National Stage Lines," the "Pilot," "Pioneer," "June Bug," and "Defiance." Not one of them cared for mud or dust, for horses or men, if only it could be the first to reach its destination.

FIG. 37. BRIDGE AND MONUMENT, NATIONAL ROAD, NEAR WHEELING, WEST VIRGINIA

There must have been dust enough, for twenty coaches with their many horses sometimes followed one another in a close line.

Henry Clay was one of the chief advocates of this road, and a monument built in his honor may be seen near the bridge, shown in Fig. 37. It is a few miles east of Wheeling. At Brownsville a small stream called Dunlap's creek flows into the Monongahela from the east. Over it is an iron bridge on the line of the National Road. According to a story told in Brownsville, Henry Clay was once overturned as he was riding through the creek before the bridge was built. As he gathered

THE NATIONAL ROAD

himself up he was heard to say, "Clay and mud shall not be mixed here again." The story goes that he went on immediately to Washington and got an order for the building of the bridge.

Whether this be true or not, it is certain that he and many other statesmen traveled over the National Road. They could not have private cars, nor did they go in drawing-room coaches, as we can if we choose. Anybody might chance to sit beside these men of national fame, as day after day they rode through the valleys and over the mountains, stopping at the wayside hotels for food and rest.

Some of the old hotels, tollhouses, and bridges, as they look to-day, are shown in the illustrations in this chapter. The road itself was long ago given up to the different states and counties through which it runs, but it still tells to the traveler who goes over it many a story of the life of a hundred years ago.

CHAPTER IX

THE BALTIMORE AND OHIO RAILROAD

Even after the Erie canal was built and long lines of boats were carrying the grain and other products of the West to New York, the men of Virginia and Maryland did not give up the notion of still making the trade of the western country come their way. They planned the Chesapeake and Ohio canal, to reach the Ohio river, and thought that other canals across the state of Ohio would let them into lake Erie. By the Ohio river they would connect with New Orleans and the upper Mississippi river, and through lake Erie they could reach the towns and farms that border lake Huron, lake Michigan, and lake Superior.

A canal along the Potomac valley had been talked of several years before the Revolution, when Richard Henry Lee laid a plan for it before the Assembly of Virginia. Doubtless others thought of it too, as of the Erie canal, long before it was made. At the end of the War of the Revolution Washington made a long journey into the wild woods of New York. He went to the source of the Susquehanna at Otsego lake, visited the portage between the Mohawk and Wood creek, and saw for himself that New York had a great chance for navigation and trade. But he had a natural love for his own Virginia, and he

THE BALTIMORE AND OHIO RAILROAD 99

did not intend to let New York go ahead of his native state. His journeys across the mountains as a surveyor and as a soldier gave him a knowledge of the Ohio country, and as he had himself taken up much good land there, he wished to have an easy way, by land or water, from the sea to the rich Ohio valley. So he thought much about a canal to run by the side of the Potomac, and he joined with others who felt as he did to form the

FIG. 38. MOUNT ROYAL STATION, BALTIMORE AND OHIO RAILROAD, BALTIMORE

Potomac Company. They started a canal, but they found so much in the way that they were not able to go far with it.

The plan for a canal came up again twenty years after Washington died, and in 1823 a charter was given for building the Chesapeake and Ohio canal. New York had then been six years at work on the Erie canal and would finish it in two years more. If the Virginia and Maryland people had known that most of them would be dead before their canal was half done, and that it would never be really finished, they would not have undertaken it.

They did not begin the work until five years later, in 1828. Then a great crowd came together at Georgetown, now a part of Washington, on the Potomac, to see the first earth thrown out. President John Quincy

FIG. 39. CHESAPEAKE AND OHIO CANAL, CUMBERLAND

Adams made the principal speech and then took a spade to begin the digging. The spade hit a root and would not go into the soil. The President set down his foot more firmly, but still the spade would not move. At last, determined to succeed, he pulled off his coat for the job. The crowd liked this and cheered loudly, while Mr. Adams accomplished what he had set out to do.

THE BALTIMORE AND OHIO RAILROAD

On this very day something else was going on at Baltimore, forty miles away. Baltimore was not on the Potomac, but her people did not propose to be left out of the western trade on that account. After much disputing a charter had been granted for building what became one of the most famous, as it is one of the oldest, American railways, — the Baltimore and Ohio. Hence Baltimore had a celebration of her own on this same Fourth of July, 1828.

They did not have the President of the United States to help them, but they fared very well. They had great faith in what they were doing, and doubtless would have shouted even louder had they known what a great railroad they were starting and what a hard time the canal people would have.

There was only one man remaining of all the patriots who had signed the Declaration of Independence almost fifty years before. This was Charles Carroll of Carrollton, and he was the guest of Baltimore on that day. A prayer was offered, the Declaration was read, and after an officer of the railway company had spoken Mr. Carroll removed the first earth. As if nature would be kind to an old man, no root made his work hard; and the superstitious may say that the President's toilsome digging over in Georgetown was a bad omen for that enterprise. It is easier to look back than to see into the future.

Both canal and railway went on building, but as they needed nearly the same route in some places, they did not get on well together. The canal was located in the state of Maryland, along the north bank of the Potomac. This was done in some measure because a large part of the water which would be needed for the canal came down from the uplands on the north side. It took twenty-three years to dig the trench as far as Cumberland, so that it was 1851 before boats could run between Cumberland and tide water. The original plan of carrying the canal beyond Cumberland and across the mountains was never carried out.

Just below the point where Wills creek enters the Potomac there is a dam, and from the pond so made the water is taken into the upper end of the canal. Much traffic has passed up and down the canal, but, on the whole, it has not paid for the cost of building and repairing. Sometimes it has been out of use, and a few months ago the state of Maryland sold it for a small sum to the Wabash Railway Company.

The *North American Review* has been published for a long time. At least seventy-five years ago this magazine printed two articles on the Baltimore and Ohio Railroad. By reading them we can see how the intelligent people of that time felt about building it.

In favor of the proposed railroad they said, first, that it would not be closed by ice for several months each year, as the Erie canal and the rivers were. Secondly, they reminded the public that Baltimore is two hundred miles nearer the Ohio navigation than New York is, and one hundred miles nearer than Philadelphia. Thirdly, they argued that New Orleans was a long way off, and its climate hot and unhealthful. Provisions sent by that route would be likely to spoil, and the traders taking the goods down the river might fall sick. Further, the rivers in a dry summer would be too low for navigation.

FIG. 40. HIGHEST POINT ON BALTIMORE AND OHIO RAILROAD, AT SAND PATCH, PENNSYLVANIA

Nor did Baltimore people think that the Erie canal could get much trade except from regions close to lake Erie, and they had noticed that lands not far from the canal still sent a good deal of produce down the Susquehanna river to Baltimore. There was no port south of them that was so good as theirs; in short, they showed a very proper pride in their own home and a conviction that Baltimore was as good as any other American city, if not, perhaps, a little better.

They said also that the lime used for building in the city of Washington was brought all the way from Rhode Island, while there was a great abundance of good limestone in their own mountains, although it could not be carried by wagons. There was coal also, in seams so thick and wide that it could never be used up, but there was no way of getting it down to the sea where it would run factories, smelt iron, and propel the new steamships that so soon would make the ocean a well-traveled highway. Slate also was to be had, and marble, and gypsum, and timber, but these could not be brought to the towns where they might be used. There was, moreover, much iron ore all along the proposed route, and we all know that iron is the most important of the metals.

It had long before been learned that there were many fish in Chesapeake bay, and that New England was not to have the fishing business all to herself. Better even than this, there were then, as there are now, places under the shallow waters where countless oysters lived and multiplied. It was said, even in 1827, that if there could be a railroad to carry things quickly, oysters might be sent to people living far from the sea.

Baltimore's notion of swift carrying was much like that of the Erie canal packet owners. Trains could go four miles an hour, and thus goods might be sent from Baltimore to the Ohio river in sixty-two and one-half hours. Some hopeful people thought that the speed might even be raised to eight miles an hour. When cars run at that rate in these days we begin to talk about getting out and pushing the engine.

The builders of the railroad had what seem to us curious ideas of laying a foundation for the track. They dug a trench in some places, putting into it broken stone, and on this they laid long slabs of stone, or "stone rails." On these, in their turn, the iron rails were riveted down. Until car springs were invented the jolting must have been like that of a farm wagon.

Even when the track was finished no decision had been made as to how the cars were to be moved. Mr. Hulbert, in one of his stories of historic highways, tells of several experiments which were made. Some one invented a locomotive in which a horse was to tread an endless belt and thus make the machine go, carrying with it the horse and dragging the cars. On one trip, when several newspaper men were present to report the trial, the train ran into a cow and they were all tipped out and tumbled down a bank. The method did not have much praise in the papers. Sails were also tried, and one car which was thus moved by wind was called *Æolus*. This car, with its mast and other ship-like rigging, made much talk, but that was all. And no one could quite see how it would ever be possible to draw a car on a curved track. This meant much, for it was out of the question to build a railway through the mountains without many curves, and some of them rather short ones. But there were those who thought that if a curved road were possible, it would be a good thing because the engineer could occasionally look back along the line and see how his train was coming on.

FIG. 41. LOOKING DOWN THE POTOMAC FROM HARPERS FERRY

Maryland on the left; West Virginia on right and in foreground; Virginia in the distance; Baltimore and Ohio Railroad and Chesapeake and Ohio canal at the left; Shenandoah river enters under bridge on the right

But steam was to win the day. Mr. Peter Cooper had a locomotive, called *Tom Thumb*, built in 1829, and an old picture shows an exciting race between this little engine and a horse car. The steam car won the race, and it is now to be seen whether or not electricity will drive steam out of business on the railways.

THE BALTIMORE AND OHIO RAILROAD

By 1833 the road was laid as far as Harpers Ferry, a place made lively by armies and guns in the Civil War. It is a rugged old town, built near the spot where the Shenandoah joins the Potomac, and both together have cut a fine gorge through the Blue Ridge. To-day as one stands in the upper part of the village and looks down through the great gorge, he sees the bridge and tracks and trains of the Baltimore and Ohio, and the channel of the Chesapeake and Ohio canal (Fig. 41). The railway outstripped the canal, for the road was finished to Cumberland in 1842, nine years before canal boats floated into that place; and in 1853 the first train rolled into Wheeling, on the Ohio river.

Another part of the road now runs farther north to Pittsburg and leads on to Chicago, while yet another passes south to Cincinnati and St. Louis. Eastward the main line runs to Philadelphia and stops at the Whitehall terminal in New York City. These long lines, with many spurs and side lines, make up the Baltimore and Ohio Railway system, which, like the Pennsylvania and the New York Central, joins the seaports of the Atlantic coast with the fields and cities of the Mississippi, and carries in either direction the rich mineral products of the intervening mountains.

Like her neighbors on the Atlantic, Baltimore stretches out her hands to sea and land. The city was begun in 1730, at which time a Mr. Carroll sold the land for it at forty shillings an acre. When Washington first went to the Ohio there were only twenty-five houses in Baltimore, but in 1770 there were twenty thousand people, and the new city was drawing trade from Philadelphia.

In 1826, when the Erie canal was building, Baltimore had become a city of sixty thousand inhabitants. Now it has more than half a million people, and is the sixth American city. In foreign trade, however, it stands third, and its docks are busy places. The Hamburg-American, the North-German Lloyd, and the Red Star lines all send regular steamers between Baltimore and Europe, and hundreds of others sail to ports on our own

FIG. 42. COKE OVENS AT MEYERSDALE, PENNSYLVANIA

coast, to the West Indies, and to South America. Baltimore builds ships as well as sails them, to carry the corn, flour, and meat of the prairies and the great plains to foreign lands, and to bring back their products in exchange. Where there are railways and ships there are always merchants and factories. Out of the gains of trade a Baltimore merchant built one of the most famous of our schools, the Johns Hopkins University.

There has been no more important factor in the development of the United States than is found in the

THE BALTIMORE AND OHIO RAILROAD 109

great railway systems, which, by linking all sections together, give unity and strength to the whole fabric of our government. Washington's dreams of his country's future are already overtopped by her actual achievements, and the most hopeful among those who first saw the advantages of steam engines could hardly have looked forward to the swift transportation of to-day.

In the year 1901 an American ship and American railway trains ran a great race to London over land and sea. The start was from Australia and the distance was more than thirteen thousand miles. The race was not against other ships and other trains, but against time. The mail from Sydney in New South Wales usually went by the Red sea and the Suez canal, a route which is a thousand miles shorter than is the Pacific route, and which took thirty-five days and a few hours. It happened on August 13, in the morning, that three hundred and sixty-seven sacks of important mail for London were piled on the dock, beside which lay a new American ship, the *Ventura*. Because no good British ship was at hand that morning, the post-office authorities thought that they would let the vessel with the Stars and Stripes carry the mail. She did carry it, and on the evening of September 2 she laid down the bags on the pier at San Francisco.

The American railroads tried their hand at carrying the British mail. The Southern Pacific took it swiftly across to Ogden, in Utah. The Union Pacific seized it, two hours late, and said that the time should be made up. The train raced a thousand miles to Omaha and made up some of the time but not all. Then it was off for Chicago, where the Lake Shore road had a "special" ready to overtake the Fast Mail. It ran two hundred and forty-four miles in two hundred and sixty-five and a half minutes, and did overtake it. Then came

FIG. 43. THE OBSERVATION END, BALTIMORE AND OHIO RAILROAD

Buffalo, New York, Queenstown, and London. The carriers in that great city started out with the mail early in the morning of September 14. If the bags had come by the shorter route under the British flag, they would not have reached London until September 16. This is what great railways and great ships do in our time, — they make neighbors of all men.

CHAPTER X

CITIES OF THE OHIO VALLEY

If we look at a map, we shall see that the Allegheny river flows southward from New York into western Pennsylvania. The Monongahela river, rising among the rough highlands of West Virginia, sends its waters toward the north, and the two great streams join to form the Ohio, which flows on far to the southwest. All together they are like wide-spreading branches of an apple tree uniting with the gnarled old trunk.

In the great crotch of the tree Pittsburg is snugly placed. A narrow point of flat land lies between the rivers just before they come together to make the Ohio, and back of this point, to the east, rise steep hills. Across the Allegheny and across the Monongahela the banks rise sharply for several hundred feet, and there too, wherever the slope is not too steep for houses to stand, tens of thousands of busy people have their homes.

The rivers are crossed by many bridges and are full of boats. Up and down for miles their banks are smoky and noisy with furnaces, and at night the iron mills light up the valley with wonderful torches of flame leaping into the black sky. If the great towns clustered within an hour's ride were counted in, Pittsburg would now have a million people. Only a hundred years ago

112   FROM TRAIL TO RAILWAY

she was, like many other cities in the New World, a humble village between two rivers. As early as 1730 white men journeyed here to trade with the Indians, who could come from any part of the western country in their canoes. Washington stood here November 24, 1753,

FIG. 44. OLD BLOCKHOUSE, PITTSBURG

and in his description of the place wrote, " I think it extremely well situated for a fort, as it has absolute command of both rivers." Men were to need forts for a long time in that country, and the one which was soon built on this site had a stirring history. In 1758 it was recaptured from the French and named for England's

CITIES OF THE OHIO VALLEY

prime minister, Pitt. Hence we have Pittsburgh, which is the old spelling, but it is now common to drop the *h*, and write it Pittsburg.

The old blockhouse of brick, which is still standing, was built in 1764. Washington came back to the spot in 1770, and found here about twenty houses, used by men who were trading with the Indians. Arthur Lee, in 1784, thought that the place would "never be very considerable," but he was not a good prophet. In 1816 it had become a city and has been steadily gaining in importance since that time. Not much more than fifty years later an historian of Pittsburg said that if Mr. Lee could then come back, he would find a city bigger than the six largest cities and towns in the Old Dominion.

The secret of Pittsburg's success is in its location. Many years ago it was called "the gate of the West," and through it has gone much of the trade between the East and the lands beyond the mountains. Even from New York the pioneers came by land and water to the head of the Ohio, an undertaking by no means easy in those days. A prominent man in Pittsburg once contracted with the government to send provisions to Oswego, and as he wished to make the long journey as profitable as he could, he packed the provisions in strong barrels that would hold salt. When these were emptied they were filled for the return trip with Onondaga salt and carried by lake Ontario to the Niagara river below the falls. They were then taken around the falls and across the lake to Erie, up French creek, over the portage, and at length by boat to Pittsburg. It was a roundabout way, but the enterprising dealer sold salt in

Pittsburg for half the price charged by the packers who brought it by rough mountain roads from the East.

Improvements in methods of transportation caused an increase in business activity. By the Pittsburg pike, by the canal with its Portage Railway, and finally by the Pennsylvania Railroad, trade was coming from Philadelphia. Not less promptly did the men of Baltimore and the Virginians reach Pittsburg by the trail, the National Road, and the Baltimore and Ohio Railroad. Because Pittsburg stood at the head of the Ohio it was a door to the whole Mississippi valley, and men and goods quickly found their way to it. Once there a boat would take them over thousands of miles of river, or to New Orleans and the open sea.

Henry Clay used to tell in Congress a good story about Pittsburg. He said that a ship built at Pittsburg sailed down the river, through the gulf, across the Atlantic, into the Mediterranean, and anchored at Leghorn. The captain handed his papers to the officer of the customhouse, who did not credit them. "Sir," said he, "your papers are forged; there is no such port as Pittsburg in the world; your vessel must be confiscated." Though the captain was frightened, he pulled out a map and taught the Italian official a lesson in geography, making him understand at last that one could sail a thousand miles up the Mississippi and another thousand up the Ohio, and that there was such a port as Pittsburg.

The first boats on the Ohio river were the light bark canoes of the red men. These could sail in almost any water, but they were easily broken and could carry only light loads. When white men began to throng the river

FIG. 45. PITTSBURG

and wanted to carry their families, household furniture, tools, grain, and all the produce of the land, they needed something larger and stronger. At first they built barges, which were little more than great boxes made water-tight. These they loaded and steered down the stream as best they could. They did not expect to bring them back, for such boats could not be pushed against the current. Hence the barge builders at Pittsburg always had work, for a new one had to be provided for each fresh cargo.

Later men began to make keel boats, in which they could not only go downstream but could also, by poling, make a return voyage. These boats were about fifty feet long and could carry twenty tons or more. Along the sides were "running boards," where the men went up and down with their setting poles to drive the boat against the current. The space between the running boards was covered over to form a kind of cabin. It was not an easy task to pole one of these boats up a rapid, and the life on the river was a life of toil.

During the last twenty years before 1800, or while Washington was President, a wealthy merchant of Philadelphia took up traffic on the Ohio. He sent dry goods and other merchandise overland to Pittsburg, thence down the Ohio in a barge, and up the Mississippi to Kaskaskia in Illinois, which was at that time an important town. Here the cargo was exchanged for skins of bear, deer, buffalo, and other animals, to be taken up the Ohio and sent from Pittsburg to Philadelphia.

It took time to trade in this way. A summer was needed to go down to New Orleans and back again with

CITIES OF THE OHIO VALLEY 117

a keel boat or a barge. When a boat came up "with furs from St. Louis; cotton from Natchez; hemp, tobacco, and saltpeter from Maysville; or sugar and cotton from New Orleans and Natchez, it was a wonder to the many, and drew vast crowds to see and rejoice over it."

One of the river men, Captain Shreve, once took his boat from New Orleans up to Louisville in twenty-five days. The people celebrated this remarkable achievement and gave the captain a public dinner. No doubt they made as much ado as we should now make if a ship should go from New York to Liverpool in three days. They were quite right to make a feast in honor of the occasion, for the time commonly allowed for the journey had been three months.

The flatboat, which for years was used in river traffic, was about forty feet long, twelve feet wide, and eight feet deep. It had a flat bottom and was handled by means of three oars on each side. Two of these were called sweeps, and were almost as long as the boat itself. At the stern was a still longer steering oar. When the water rose in the autumn these boats carried loads of produce and bore thousands of families who were seeking homes farther west.

Old and young with their household treasures, which often included the cow, sailed down in these rude house boats to some chosen spot in the distant wilderness. It was in a boat like these that the tall and awkward young man, Abraham Lincoln, made a voyage to New Orleans and first saw something of the outside world.

Redstone was an old name for Brownsville, where the National Road crossed the Monongahela, and many boats started from here in early days. It is said that an old boatman was once hailed by a seeker after information. "Where are you from?" was the first question. "Redstone," was the answer. "What is your lading?" "Millstones." "What is your captain's name?" "Whetstone." "Where are you bound?" "For Limestone." The interesting part of the story is that these answers were all true.

Large as the traffic was by the flatboats, it was greatly increased when steamboats began to run on the rivers. No other craft could hope to compete with these.

The boatmen owed a grudge to the steamboat, just as the pack-horse men had hated the Conestoga wagon, for they saw that their trade was lost, and it was hard to try to make a living in some other way. For many years the great passenger boats reigned supreme on the rivers of the West, but at last they in turn were forced to give way to the railroads. Such boats still run on the Ohio and the Mississippi, but men do not travel on them when they wish to go quickly.

Railroad cars, however, do not take the place of some boats on the Ohio. Look out on the Monongahela at Pittsburg and you may see large fields of boats, — many acres of barges, for there are barges on the river still, though they do not look like the old ones. They are of great size and are sometimes made of steel. The coal, taken from the hill out of which it is dug, is run on a trestle along the river and dumped into one of these boats. At Pittsburg the barges wait for the water to rise to a "coal-boat" stage, — that is, until there is a depth of at least eight feet all the way down the river.

Then a number of barges are lashed together and a steamboat pushes them down the stream. The water often comes up suddenly, and the coal must be rushed to market while the high water lasts. A single towboat sometimes takes to New Orleans several acres of coal from the great Pittsburg coal seam. This lies flat under the hilltops and is mined from the edges where the rivers

FIG. 46. COAL BARGES, PITTSBURG

have cut down through the coal, far into the beds of rock that lie below.

On the Monongahela the United States owns fifteen dams with locks, and the river is thus "slacked" far up into West Virginia. The dams change the river into a series of long, still ponds, which are deep enough to float the coal barges. Below Pittsburg, in the Ohio, is another dam which sets the water back and makes a harbor for the city.

There is no coal to send down the Allegheny, but there are logs to be rafted, and there is much oil, for the river flows through the petroleum region around Oil City. Some of this is taken to refineries at Pittsburg and made ready for use. Much natural gas is obtained by boring and is used in the city for warming houses and for cooking.

A cloud of smoke from the soft coal burned in so many shops and furnaces hangs over the lower parts of Pittsburg and has given it the name of "The Smoky

FIG. 47. PITTSBURG AT NIGHT

City." James Parton says that on the first morning of his visit there he felt sure that he was rising very early, for the street lamps were all burning and he ate his breakfast in a room lighted by gas. As the room was filled with people, he thought Pittsburg was very enterprising, and himself along with it, but he was quite taken aback when he looked at his watch and found that it was almost nine o'clock. Darker even than the streets are the

CITIES OF THE OHIO VALLEY

"rooms" in which thousands of miners, within a few miles of the city, dig out coal with their picks and shovels.

If one rides into Pittsburg by night, he will see something finer than fireworks. The train is likely to whirl him past long rows of fiery ovens in which coal is being made into coke. And in many towns near by, as well as

FIG. 48. FURNACES NEAR PITTSBURG

along the rivers by the city itself, the jets of flame will show iron furnaces and steel mills, with grimy workmen moving about in the strange light.

The iron ore for these furnaces is brought from many parts of the country, but chiefly from the lands around lake Superior. It is shipped down the lakes in large steamers and loaded into cars at Cleveland or some other port on lake Erie. Instead of carrying the coal to the ore, the ore is thus brought to the coal, without which it could not be worked. The reason for this is that Pittsburg is much nearer the places where most of the iron is to be used. If the coal of Pennsylvania were taken to the iron mines of Minnesota and the furnaces built there, much of the iron and steel would have to be carried back a long way to Boston, New York, Philadelphia, and other parts of the East.

Glass mills form an important part of the city's industries and have been in operation for a long time. Bottle glass is manufactured here, besides three fourths of all the plate glass of the United States. Perhaps it is because bottles are made in Pittsburg that we find here also the largest cork factory in the world.

Pittsburg is proud of the fact that she handles more tons of freight in a year than any other city in the world. Indeed, the tonnage is greater than that of New York and Chicago taken together.

The old "point" between the rivers is filled with tall buildings. Inclined railways run up the steep bluffs on the further side of each river and lead to the beautiful streets and the homes where many of the people live. For Pittsburg is not all coal and furnaces and smoke, but has fine churches, the great Carnegie Library and Museum, and many schools. But it is mostly because of the coal and the rivers that we find here a splendid city.

Sixty-three miles down the Ohio river, on its left bank, is Wheeling, the largest city in West Virginia. The business streets lie close to the Ohio, and the houses

CITIES OF THE OHIO VALLEY 123

extend up the steep slope to the east, while over a high ridge comes the old National Road from the valley of Wheeling creek. Wheeling was the goal of many heavily laden wagons in the days of the pike, and because of the river and many railroads has a large trade to-day. It was settled in 1770 and is one of the oldest towns on the river.

On the north bank of the great stream, in the southwest corner of Ohio, is the largest city on the river. As late as 1900 Cincinnati had a few thousand more people than Pittsburg, but a "greater Cincinnati" would not be so large as a "greater Pittsburg."

In Cincinnati, as in Pittsburg, men do business on the low grounds by the river, where offices and mills and shops crowd one another, and the smoke of soft coal hangs as a cloud above. Business hours over, the well-to-do merchants climb out of the grimy town to the top of the bluffs, and there find, in a clearer air and along open and beautiful avenues, their comfortable homes. Down town the turbulent river sometimes comes up forty or fifty feet beyond its usual level and makes trouble in the busy city, but Mt. Auburn and Walnut Hills are disturbed neither by smoke nor by floods.

Rivers do not often flow in straight lines, and it is very common for them to change their courses along their flood plains. This habit of shifting belongs alike to great and small streams, whether the Mississippi or the brook in the meadow. The Ohio, like other rivers, often writes the letter S, and in so doing at this point has swung off from its old north bank, leaving a low plain with room enough for a hundred thousand people to carry on their business. There is always some good reason which has led to the settlement and growth of a town, and the history of Cincinnati shows no exception.

It was in early winter, 1788, when cakes of ice were already floating on the river, that a number of men sailing downstream stopped here and began a settlement. The place was not readily named. It is said that the matter was left to a frontier schoolmaster, and he did not lose the chance to show how much he knew. He saw that the Licking river comes into the Ohio on the Kentucky side just opposite. So he set down an L. He next remembered an ancient word *os*, meaning "mouth," and he put that down. Then he considered that *anti* means "opposite" and that *ville* means "town." So he wrote the whole name, — *L-os-anti-ville*, — *Losantiville*, — "the town opposite the mouth of Licking."

We might wonder whether a town with a name like that would ever grow into a great city. It did not have to try, for it was not long before General St. Clair, who had come there, made fun of the name and insisted upon a new one. He and other officers of the American army had formed a society commemorating their experience in the Revolution, and in honor of the Roman patriot Cincinnatus had called themselves the Order of Cincinnati. St. Clair thought this a good name for the town, and Cincinnati it has been since that time.

The place has its nickname also, and its people like to call it the Queen City, which seems to go very well with Beautiful River. Another name, rarely used and not very pleasing, perhaps, to those who live there, is "Porkopolis," which came from the fact that for forty years

FIG. 49. RIVER FRONT, CINCINNATI

before the American Civil War more pork packing was done in Cincinnati than anywhere else in the country.

Sir Charles Lyell, an Englishman who saw Cincinnati in 1842, speaks of the "pork aristocracy," explaining that he means the men that had grown rich by packing pork, and not the pigs that he saw running in the streets. This shows how new some of our large business centers are, though it would be a great mistake to suppose that pigs and cows now run loose in western cities. In those days such places were teaching the country how to "pack fifteen bushels of corn into a pig," and how to send the produce of the farms to distant cities or other lands in such a way as to get the most money for the least freight.

When Charles Dickens visited this country many years ago he went to Cincinnati, and spoke well of the place. This was a great compliment, for the famous English story-teller was hard to suit when he was looking at anything American. If he could come back to Cincinnati now, he might find even more to please and surprise him.

Cincinnati has always made much use of the river. There were little boats in which the owners carried notions and such things as a country store sells, peddling them from one settlement to another along the banks. There were barges and flatboats bearing families and farm produce. Then came steamboats, which carried everything, — passengers, grain, coal, merchandise, and even circuses and menageries. We can imagine the excitement among the small boys of a river town when the circus boat told of its arrival by the fierce blast of a loud steam whistle. There are steamboats yet and a busy river front, but great railroads center here, and trains run to Pittsburg and Philadelphia, Cleveland and New York, Chicago and St. Louis, Nashville and New Orleans. A vast business is done. There are many schools, and to-day Cincinnati can boast of her music, of her pictures and museums, and of the fine pottery that she makes. She has thrown off the schoolmaster's clumsy name, she has many better things than pork, and she is widely known as one of America's great cities.

An early writer says that the Ohio is "by far the noblest river in the universe." He writes this in the beginning of a history of Louisville, a book which was printed in 1819. This in itself shows that Louisville is one of the old cities of the Ohio valley. It is not so large as Cincinnati or Pittsburg, but it is the chief city of the great state of Kentucky.

The old boatmen, finding that the current was rapid at a certain point, called it the "falls of the Ohio." A ledge of hard rocks in the bed of the river caused the rapids and made it no easy task to navigate boats. Finally a canal was dug by which the rapids might be avoided at low water.

It was this ledge in the river that started the town and finally made a city out of Louisville, for boats going in either direction naturally stopped at the falls. There was another reason, too, as we shall see when we learn something of the "Wilderness Road," which crossed Kentucky from the eastern mountains and came out on the river at Louisville. Back from the river also lay the rich and fertile Blue Grass country for which Kentucky is famous.

The canal was ready to take steamboats around the ledge in 1831. Some of these boats had interesting names, such as the *Enterprise*, the *Vesuvius*, the *Comet*, the *Volcano*, the *New Orleans*, the *Cincinnati*, the *Experiment*, the *Rifleman*, and the *Rising States*.

It was a wonderful life on the river, and Louisville got her share of the gain of it, as she now shares the traffic of the railroads. To-day she is a rich and beautiful city of two hundred thousand people.

CHAPTER XI

THE GREAT VALLEY

Alexander Spotswood was a famous governor of the colony of Virginia. He was of Scottish parentage, but he was born in Morocco, where his father was a surgeon. The lad grew up to serve his country as a soldier, and was wounded by a cannon ball in a great war then going on in Europe. In 1710 the king sent him to Virginia to be governor, an office which he filled for twelve years. The people liked him, though he made some enemies because he kept his soldierly ways and did not always speak in gentle phrases. He was a kind, warm-hearted man, nevertheless, loving his family and friends. His energy, too, was well known, and he was always ready to further a new scheme.

Because he started the first iron furnaces in America he was called the "Tubal Cain of Virginia," Tubal Cain being known in sacred history as the first of metal workers. Nothing was more important to the colonists than iron, for they could not always bring tools and kettles and nails and gun metal from England. The governor showed his practical ability in other ways. He brought over Germans who knew how to raise grapes and make wine. He was interested in teaching the Indians, and at one time he sent out ships and caught

"Blackbeard," who, with his fellow-pirates, was prowling about the coast. When the young Benjamin Franklin, in Boston, heard of the capture he wrote a poem about it.

In that day nearly all of Virginia was in the "tide-water country," but Spotswood had often heard of the valley beyond the Blue Ridge. He made up his mind to go and see this region, and brought together a party to make the journey. They took their servants and pack horses and carried provisions and many bottles of the wine which the Germans had made. There was good hunting in the unbroken forest and they had all the venison and other wild meat they could have wished.

A good map of Virginia will show us Harpers Ferry, where the Potomac river runs through a deep gap in the Blue Ridge. Looking along the range to the southwest, we shall find, about eighty miles away, Swift Run Gap, not so low a pass, but one which made it easy to cross the mountains and go down into the lowlands along the Shenandoah river.

Spotswood and his friends climbed one of the peaks of the Blue Ridge and named it Mt. George, after the king. Another peak was named Alexander for the governor. Down by the Shenandoah they buried a bottle (the historian of Virginia thinks that by this time they must have had several that were empty), and in the bottle was a paper stating that they took possession in the name of the king. They called the river the Euphrates, but the name did not cling to it. We may be glad of that, for the Indian name of Shenandoah is much more musical.

FIG. 56. LURAY, SHENANDOAH VALLEY

If Spotswood had crossed the lowlands, he would have found himself among other mountains running parallel to the Blue Ridge. Between the two ranges is the valley of the Shenandoah, or, as it is quite as often called, the valley of Virginia. The land is flat and the soil deep and rich. The soft shales and limestone of ancient higher lands have wasted away here, between the higher mountains on either side, and thus we find a valley and a fertile valley floor.

The place was wild and lonely when this band of explorers visited it, but to-day it is a country rich in interest and associations. If we go northeast we shall pass Winchester, which became famous in the Civil War. In another part of the valley is Luray, where the limestones have been dissolved under the ground, making a large cavern with beautiful stalactites. Still going northward, we shall pass Harpers Ferry on our right and cross the Potomac. On our right also, after we cross the river, is Antietam, where a severe battle was fought between Lee and McClellan. A little farther on is Hagerstown, Colonel Rochester's old home, in the state of Maryland.

The next move would take us over into Pennsylvania, through Chambersburg and Carlisle, about which we already know, and across the Susquehanna to Harrisburg. On our right, as we go up into Pennsylvania, is the low South mountain, which is the Blue Ridge continued. All this time we are in the Great Valley. The valley of Virginia is but a part of the whole, which reaches through several states and everywhere has the Blue Ridge on the southeast and other ridges of the Appalachian mountains

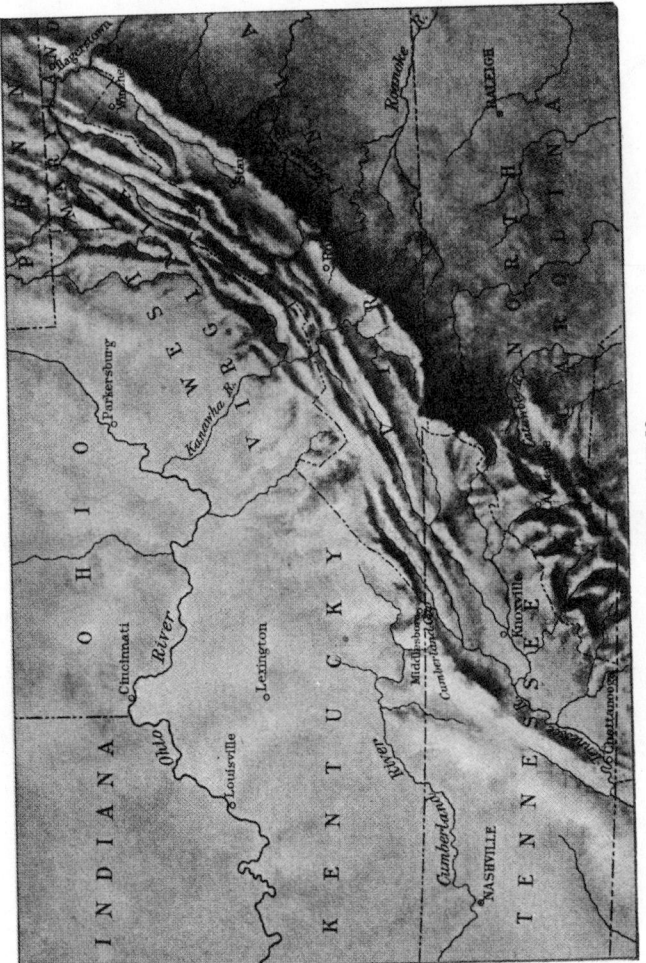

SCALE OF MILES
0 10 20 40 60 80 100

THE GREAT VALLEY

on the northwest. Every part of the valley is thickly settled and has fine houses and homes, because its soil produces good crops and makes the people prosperous.

Spotswood's journey opened the way for families from the tide-water region to settle beyond the mountains, but they were not the only settlers. It was easy for the people of the Great Valley in Pennsylvania, where the land was earlier taken up, to push to the southwest along the same valley. They found smoother traveling and better farms than if they had gone up into the mountains on the west. So we see that the valley, leading southwest, guided the stream of emigrants in that direction. The result was that the valley of Virginia was occupied partly by people entering through Pennsylvania, and partly by those who, like Spotswood, came through passes in the Blue Ridge. It was thirty years later, when most of the land was still a wilderness, that we find George Washington crossing these same mountains to survey for Lord Fairfax. His path lay between Harpers Ferry and Swift Run Gap.

In this valley, during the Civil War, "Stonewall" Jackson, Sheridan, and other well-known generals took their armies up and down, and fought a number of battles. The rich farms and full barns of the valley played no small part in the strife by furnishing food for the soldiers.

The headwaters of the James river are in the Great Valley. One branch flows southwest and another northeast. These come together and go out to the southeast by a gap in the Blue Ridge. To-day we come up the Shenandoah by the Norfolk and Western Railway, which continues along these branches of the James. Before long we reach Roanoke, a flourishing city just inside the Blue Ridge. Then follows the crossing of the New river, which flows northwest across the valley on its long course to the Ohio.

Now we are looking toward Tennessee, and the Great Valley soon takes us to several long streams which help to form the Tennessee river. The heads of these streams we shall find in Virginia, and their names are the Holston, the Clinch, and Powell's river. The Great Valley

FIG. 51. JAMES RIVER GAP IN THE BLUE RIDGE, FROM THE WEST

in this southwestern part of Virginia is really divided into several valleys by long and rather high ridges that separate these rivers.

The main line of the Southern Railway, between Washington and Knoxville, runs along the valley of the Holston river and crosses from Virginia into Tennessee at Bristol.

After we come into Tennessee the ridges that separate the streams fall away again, and we find one great valley, about forty miles wide. On the northwest the Cumberland plateau and the Cumberland mountains rise above it. On the southeast there loom up the Great Smoky mountains on the border of North Carolina. Great Smoky is only another name for the Blue

THE GREAT VALLEY

Ridge, for it is the same range, only higher and wider than it is farther north.

Although this valley is a part of the Great Valley, it is commonly called the valley of east Tennessee, its people using the home name as they do in Virginia. The Holston, the Clinch, and Powell's river are not the only branches of the Tennessee. Out of the Great Smoky mountains there flow from the east the French Broad, the Little Tennessee, and the Hiwassee. Knoxville stands a little below the place where the Holston and French Broad flow together, and Chattanooga is a hundred miles farther down, where the Tennessee, now a lordly stream, leaves the Great Valley and flows westward through a deep valley in the Cumberland plateau. This lesson in geography we must learn well, with the help of a map, and we shall then see what the pioneers did as they followed the rivers between the mountains.

It is an old road that runs from Pennsylvania to Tennessee by the valley. It took the pioneer across the Potomac through Winchester and Staunton in Virginia. Farther on was a fortified place, Fort Chissel, built in 1758, which was on the way to the Watauga Settlement and Cumberland Gap. Of Watauga we must now tell, and of the Cumberland Gap in the next chapter.

Watauga is the name of a small river which flows out of the mountains on the east, into the Great Valley, and enters the Holston. In a pleasant spot on the banks of this stream the first settlement of white men in Tennessee was made. Some of the people had come along the valley from Pennsylvania and Virginia, and others had climbed over the mountains from North Carolina because of the wrongs they had suffered there.

Many of these men and women had come from the north of Ireland. They were not of Irish but of Scotch blood, their ancestors having originally come from Scotland to make the north of Ireland their home. For this reason they are often called Scotch-Irish, but whatever we name them, we are to remember that they were sturdy and intelligent people. Conscientious and loyal Presby-

FIG. 52. HILLY FARM LANDS IN THE GREAT VALLEY, NEAR KNOXVILLE

terians they were in faith, and by nature brave and full of endurance. Their fathers had shed their blood for freedom on Scottish fields, and the sons were not likely to be frightened by a wilderness full of red savages.

Besides the Scotch-Irish, there were many Germans who had followed the valley from Pennsylvania, and there were Huguenots also, besides a few Hollanders and Swedes. A fort was built on the little river, and around this defense grew up the Watauga Settlement. There was no Tennessee in those days.

THE GREAT VALLEY 137

Many of the settlers had followed down the valleys from earlier homes in Virginia, and it never occurred to them that they were not still living in Virginia, and able to call on the colony for help. But after a time a man came to the settlement who was a surveyor, and for some reason he thought that he would run the boundary line of Virginia farther west. When he had done it, what was the surprise of every one to find that they were not in Virginia at all! If they belonged to any colony, it was to North Carolina. Unfortunately there was a lack of good government in that colony, and the prospect of belonging to it was not a pleasant one; indeed, some of the settlers had run away from North Carolina, and had felt safer because the great mountains rose between them and their former home.

There seemed nothing to do but to make a government of their own, so they formed the Watauga Association, about which writers of American history have said a good deal. It would be interesting to see a copy of the constitution that was drawn up by these backwoodsmen, but it has been lost, with little hope that it will ever be recovered. It is known, however, that there was a committee of thirteen, really a legislature. This committee chose five of their own number to form a court, which had a clerk and a sheriff and made laws for all the settlers. Roosevelt, in his *Winning of the West*, says that these pioneers were the first to build a "free and independent community" in America.

The two most important men of this little state in the wild forest show us that the settlers came from widely different places. James Robertson was one, and he came over the mountains from North Carolina. John Sevier was the other, and he came down the valley from Virginia. We shall need to know what sort of men these were.

James Robertson belonged to the Scotch-Irish people. He was not one of the very first settlers at Watauga, but came in the second year, 1770. He had no early education, and his wife, an intelligent woman, taught him to read. He went alone over the mountains, with only his horse and gun, in search of a place for a home. He found the settlers and admired the place which they had chosen, but on his way back in the fall he lost his horse and got his powder wet. He wandered about, almost starved, until he met some hunters, who helped him home. He told his neighbors of the lands in the valley, and as soon as the winter was over his own family and sixteen others started out for Watauga. He built a log house, went to work on the land, and by his wisdom and energy soon came to be a leader of the new colony.

John Sevier did not come until 1772. His father had been a settler in the Shenandoah valley, and John followed the streams, as we have traced them, to the Great Valley. He was by birth a gentleman, using that word to mean a man born of cultivated parents and familiar with the world. He was well educated and was acquainted with prominent men, such as Franklin and Madison. Both he and Robertson were good fighters, as we shall see.

It was not long before seven hundred Indian warriors, angry because the white people had made homes on their hunting grounds, stole in upon the settlement. An

THE GREAT VALLEY 139

Indian woman, Nancy Ward by name, who felt kindly toward the whites, secretly warned them of the attack, so that when the savages came they found all the men, women, and children in the fort. It was not much of a fort, but it saved their lives. The Indians kept up the attack for six days, but the colonists, led by Sevier and Robertson, held out against them and killed a number of

FIG. 53. FROM THE PINNACLE, CUMBERLAND GAP, LOOKING NORTH-EAST ALONG THE CUMBERLAND MOUNTAINS. THE GREAT VALLEY AT THE RIGHT

their braves. When nearly a week had passed the red men, tired of the siege, went off through the forest.

At one time, when some lawless whites had killed an Indian without reason, the members of the tribe were very angry and threatened to avenge the murder. Robertson, thinking that he could soften their anger, went alone among the fierce Cherokees. He told them that the Watauga people were very sorry the man had been killed, and that they would try to find and punish the murderer. As the Indians believed Robertson to be an honest man, they did as he asked them to do and the settlers were not disturbed.

The Watauga colonists had to live in a very rough and simple way. They built their cabins of logs, with what were called puncheon floors, — that is, floors made of thick, rude slabs. Frequently a big slab served for a table, three-legged stools for chairs, and a row of pegs for a wardrobe. Roosevelt says that the dress of the men was largely copied from that of the Indians, and included a fur cap, leggings of buckskin or elk hide, and a fringed hunting shirt. A heavy rifle was carried, which was usually fired from a rest.

Garments and bed clothing were made of wool, which was spun at home by the wives and daughters. The women worked hard from morning till night, and the men had many things to do. There were lands to be cleared, crops to be raised, and game to be hunted and dressed. Besides all these occupations it was necessary to keep a constant lookout for hostile savages and to have all means of defense ready in case of a sudden attack. The Indians were so crafty and deceitful that only the closest watchfulness saved the palefaces from danger and death. Sometimes an unwary hunter, hearing the gobbling of a turkey or the call of an owl, would come out into an open place only to be laid low by the red man's bullet. These experiences developed a strong and brave people.

The settlers often bartered things because they had no money, and they were ignorant of many of the ways of civilized life. Some of the frontiersmen did not know that tea leaves should be steeped and used for a drink, and tried to eat them with butter or salt.

When a boy was twelve years old he had to begin to take a man's part. A gun was given to him, and he was placed at a loophole in the fort to help keep off the savage foe. Thus the boys grew up to be real men, knowing little fear, able to take care of themselves, and helping to build one of the great states of the American Union.

CHAPTER XII

TO KENTUCKY BY THE CUMBERLAND GAP

Dr. Thomas Walker was a man of Virginia. He had attended William and Mary College, and was well educated for his times. As the agent of a land company which had a grant of new lands in Kentucky, he, with several companions, made a hard journey of six months into the wilderness. They started at Charlottesville in Virginia, went through the Blue Ridge into the Great Valley, and then followed the valley southwest. One of Walker's companions bore the name of Ambrose Powell, and as they followed one of the long streams that flow to the southwest to form the Tennessee, they named it Powell's river. His son afterwards was an officer in the Revolution, and it is said that A. P. Hill, a well-known Confederate general in the Civil War, was his great-grandson.

These were, in fact, no common men who, in the year 1750, ventured out into the forest, over the roughest trails we can imagine, among wild animals and savage men. Following down Powell's river, the travelers saw rugged mountains on their right, the Cumberland range. As they wished to explore the forests of Kentucky, they were looking for a chance to pass the mountains, and by and by they came in sight of a deep notch, cut at least a thousand feet below the top of the mountain ridge (Fig. 54).

They turned aside to this and followed it out of the Great Valley. They had to climb up about five hundred feet through a wooded ravine in order to reach the top of the pass, and there was a similar slope on the other side. This brought them to an open valley and to a

FIG. 54. CUMBERLAND GAP FROM THE EAST

river, which they followed through a gap in another mountain range, the Pineville mountains.

Dr. Walker called the first pass the Cumberland Gap, in honor of a well-known Englishman, and the name has survived even to the present day. In like manner we have the Cumberland mountains. Walker did not go far enough west to find the beautiful Kentucky lands on the Ohio river. After wandering about in the high, rough country of eastern Kentucky, he finally reached his Virginia home without having accomplished much in the service of his company.

But he had found and named what has become one of the most famous historical places in America, the Cumberland Gap. He was not the first man to go through it, for the Indians had long been familiar with it. Their trail had traversed it for no one knows how many generations. Not only did it lead directly to the open, fertile country west of the mountains, but beyond it the warrior's trail stretched northward through the woods to the Ohio river.

The Watauga Settlement was about fifty miles eastward from the Cumberland Gap. As the hardy pioneers did not make much of following a forest trail for fifty miles, the Watauga colony was next door to Kentucky, and the great gap in the Cumberland mountains was only a step farther on, either for them or for travelers to the West who might choose this route.

We must now follow the fortunes of the most famous of Kentucky hunters and pioneers, who, while he did not find or name the Cumberland Gap, often went through it, and is remembered by most people in connection with it. This man was Daniel Boone.

We could not find a better example of the movement along the Great Valley to the southwest than the life of Boone; for his childhood was spent on what was then the frontier, and his experience was like that of hundreds of others similarly reared.

Boone was born near the Schuylkill river in Pennsylvania in 1734, two years after the birth of Wăshington. This part of Pennsylvania was still on the edge of the wilderness, and from his early boyhood Boone knew all about the Indians. His family were Quakers, and he himself was quiet and thoughtful, learning to read from the Quaker wife of his eldest brother, but getting most of his education in the fields and woods. Though he could

FIG. 55. DANIEL BOONE

read, he spelled almost as badly as did Nicholas Herkimer. Boone had some experience as a blacksmith, which, his biographer says, taught him how to mend his traps and guns. He used to hunt in the woods in winter, helping thus to feed the family, and with the skins which he took to Philadelphia he bought powder, lead, and hunting knives.

When Boone was about sixteen years old his family decided to move. They went along the Great Valley, as many were doing in those days, crossed the Potomac, and traveled far through the valley of Virginia. Then they turned east, crossed the Blue Ridge, and made a home in the valley of the Yadkin river in North Carolina. They were thus east of the mountains, and across, to the west, was the Watauga Settlement.

While his home was in North Carolina Boone had an experience which helped him to be a rugged pioneer, for he went up to Virginia and across the mountains with General Braddock, serving as wagoner and blacksmith. He found himself in dangerous quarters in the battle, where many of the teamsters were shot, but he managed to cut his horses loose, mounted one of them, and escaped.

On this expedition he made friends with John Finley, and together they planned to go at some future time to Kentucky by the Cumberland Gap and enjoy the fine hunting in the forests of the West. Finley had already made a journey down to the falls of the Ohio river.

At home Boone lived, like all others in those valleys, in a small log cabin chinked with clay and warmed by a large fireplace, in which, says his biographer, "the young wife (for Boone was now married) cooked simple meals of corn mush, pumpkins, squashes, beans, potatoes, and pork, or wild meat of many kinds."

Boone spent his time in farming, working at the forge, and hunting; but he liked hunting best, and was never

TO KENTUCKY BY THE CUMBERLAND GAP 147

so happy as in the thick forest alone with his gun. He often went on long hunting trips, returning with bear's meat, venison, bear's oil, and furs, the last to be sold for other things needed at home.

In 1767 Boone and one or two friends made a hunting tour into Kentucky, though they did not know they were so far west as that. As they were kept there by

FIG. 56. PINEVILLE GAP, WHERE THE CUMBERLAND RIVER PASSES PINEVILLE MOUNTAIN A FEW MILES BEYOND CUMBERLAND GAP

heavy snows, they camped at a "salt lick" and lived by shooting the buffaloes and other animals that came to get the salt.

The hunters returned to their homes in the spring and did not go out until 1769. Meantime John Finley was peddling in that south land, and one day surprised Boone, and himself, too, by knocking at the door of Boone's cabin. He made the hardy pioneer a long visit, and in the spring, having talked it all over many times, they set out for Kentucky.

They crossed the Blue Ridge and the Great Valley and came to Cumberland Gap. This was Boone's first journey to the great pass. It is pleasant now to stand in the gap at the top of the pass and think of the time when Boone with his hunting friends made their way up from the east and went happily down through the woods to the strange country on the west.

At one time they were taken by Indians, who plundered their camp and stole all their furs. Most of the party were discouraged and went back to the settlements, but Boone and one companion were angry at their loss and determined to stay and make it good. This was like Boone, who knew nothing of fear, and who did not easily give up what he wanted to do.

He made several trips to Kentucky and greatly liked the new country. At length, having decided to take his family with him and make his home there, he became the leader of the pioneers that went out under the Transylvania Company, as it was called.

They built a fort and founded a place named Boonesborough, after the great hunter. But he was much more than a hunter, being now a military commander and doing surveying also for people who were taking up tracts of new land. Houses and forts were built, forests were cleared, and crops were raised. Such was the beginning of the state of Kentucky.

It was not all simple and pleasant work, however. In 1768, the year before Daniel Boone and John Finley went through the Cumberland Gap, a great company of

Indians had gathered at Fort Stanwix, which we remember from the battle of Oriskany, and by a treaty had given to the English the rights to the Kentucky region. But the powerful Cherokees of the southern mountains were not at Fort Stanwix, and they had something to say about the settlement of Kentucky lands. So Boone called them together at a great meeting on the Watauga river, and bought the Kentucky forests from them. This was the time when an old chief said to Boone, "Brother, we have given you a fine land, but I believe you will have much trouble settling it." The old Indian was right, — they did have much trouble. Cabins were burnt, and settlers were slain with gun and tomahawk, but Boone and many others with him would admit no failure. People began to pour in through the Cumberland Gap, until more forests were cleared, the towns grew larger, and the Indians, who do not like to fight in the open country, drew back to the woods and the mountains.

Boone marked out the trail which was afterwards known as the Wilderness road. It had also been known as Boone's trail, Kentucky road, Virginia road, and Caintuck Hog road. A man who went out with Boone in one of his expeditions to Kentucky kept a diary, and in it he gives the names of some of the new settlers. One of these was Abraham Hanks, who was Abraham Lincoln's grandfather. It was no easy journey that these men made to Kentucky, and no easy life that they found when they got there, but they planted the first American state beyond the mountains, and the rough pioneers who lived in cabins and ate pork, pumpkins, and corn bread were the ancestors of some of our most famous men.

150   FROM TRAIL TO RAILWAY

The Wilderness road has never been a good one, and is no more than any other byroad through a rough country to-day. Sometimes the early travelers, who always went in companies for safety, would be too tired to go on until they had stopped to rest and to get cheer by singing hymns and saying prayers. But they made the best of

FIG. 57. CORNFIELD NEAR CUMBERLAND GAP

it, for they knew that they were going to a fine country, which would repay them for their sufferings.

Boone and five other men were once in camp by a stream, and were lucky enough to have with them the story of *Gulliver's Travels*. One of the young men, who had been hearing the book read by the camp fire, came in one night bearing a couple of scalps that he had taken from a pair of savages. He told his friends that "he had been that day to Lulbegrud and had killed two

Brobdingnags in their capital." The stream near which it happened is still called Lulbegrud creek. These wilderness men made the best of things, and though they worked hard and fought often, they were a cheerful and happy company. They were not spoiled by having too many luxuries, and they did not think that the world owed them a living without any effort on their part.

Beginning about the time of the Declaration of Independence, many people found the way to Kentucky by the Great Valley, the Cumberland Gap, and the Wilderness road. When fifteen years had gone by there were seventy thousand people in Kentucky, along the Ohio river. Not all had come by the gap, for some had sailed down the river; but they all helped to plant the new state.

Moreover in fighting off the Indians from their own cabins and cornfields they had protected the frontiers of Virginia and others of the older states, so that Kentucky was a kind of advance guard beyond the mountains, and led the way for Ohio, Indiana, Tennessee, and other great states in the West and South.

Down in the heart of Kentucky, by the Ohio river, is a land long known as the Kentucky Blue Grass region. The " blue grass," as it is called, grows luxuriantly here, as do grain and tobacco, for the soils, made by the wasting of limestone, are rich and fertile. Wherever the soil and climate are good, crops are large and the people thrive. They have enough to eat and plenty to sell, and thus they can have good homes, many comforts, books, and education.

If the pioneers had had to settle in the high, rough, eastern parts of Kentucky, it would not have been worth while to suffer so much to get there; but they were on the way to the Blue Grass country. Even before the coming of the white man there were open lands which, perhaps by Indian fires, had lost their cover of trees. Such lands are often called prairies. These prairies, however, were not so flat as those of Illinois, and they were bordered by groves and forests. There were fine streams everywhere, and near by was the great Ohio, ready to serve as a highway toward Philadelphia or New Orleans.

FIG. 58. KENTUCKY BLUE GRASS

The Wilderness road came out on the river at the falls of the Ohio, and here, as we have learned, a city began to spring up, partly because of the falls and partly because of the Blue Grass region lying back of it. In this region we find the state capital, and here, along the roads, may be seen old mansions belonging to well-to-do descendants of the plucky men who came in by the Wilderness road or steered their flatboats down the Ohio.

If we go back to Cumberland Gap, we shall see that many things have happened since Boone's time. In the pass and on the Pinnacle, a thousand feet above on the north, are ridges of earth, which show where busy shovels

TO KENTUCKY BY THE CUMBERLAND GAP 153

threw up defenses in the Civil War; for armies passed this way between Kentucky and the valley of Tennessee, and made the gap an important point to be seized and held.

The road through the gap is still about as bad a path as one could find. Near it on the east side of the mountains is yet to be seen a furnace of rough stones, built in those early days for smelting iron. But there is little else to remind us of that far-off time. To-day you may, if you choose, pass the mountains without climbing through the gap, for trains go roaring through a tunnel a mile long, while the echo of the screaming whistles rolls along the mountain sides.

On the flat grounds just inside the gap is Middlesboro, a town of several thousand people, with wide streets and well-built shops and houses. Only a few miles away are coal mines from which thousands of tons of coal are dug, and this is one reason why the railroads are here. There are endless stores of fuel under these highlands, and men are breaking into the wilderness as fast as they can.

FIG. 59. THREE STATES MONUMENT, CUMBERLAND GAP

But if we climb through the gap as Boone did, or ride a horse to the Pinnacle, we may look out upon the wonderful valley below, stretching off to the foot of the Great

Smoky mountains, whose rugged tops carry our eyes far over into North Carolina. Or we may turn the other way and follow Boone's trail to the Blue Grass. Down in the gap is a rough, weather-beaten pillar of limestone about three feet high and leaning as the picture shows (Fig. 59). It is almost, but not quite, where three states come together, for it is here, at the Cumberland Gap, that the corners of Virginia and Kentucky meet on the edge of Tennessee.

CHAPTER XIII

FRONTIER SOLDIERS AND STATESMEN

Not long before the Revolution began some treacherous whites in the western country had murdered the whole family of the friendly Indian chief, Logan. This aroused the tribes and led to war. A piece of flat land runs out between the two streams where the Great Kanawha river joins the Ohio, in what is now West Virginia. Here, on a day early in October, 1774, twelve hundred frontiersmen were gathered under the command of an officer named Andrew Lewis.

These backwoods soldiers were attacked by a thousand of the bravest Indian warriors, commanded by Cornstalk, a Shawnee chief. It was a fierce struggle and both sides lost many men, but the pioneers held their ground, and the red men, when they had had enough fighting, went away. This battle at Point Pleasant finished what is sometimes known as Lord Dunmore's War, so called because it was carried on under Lord Dunmore, the last governor that the English king sent out to Virginia.

The successful white men were now free to go down the Ohio river and settle on the Kentucky lands. Among the patriots fighting for their frontier homes were our old friends James Robertson and John Sevier of Watauga, and another young man, Isaac Shelby. We are to hear again about all these, for they were men likely to be found whenever something important was to be done.

The Great Kanawha is the same stream that we have called the New river where it crosses the Great Valley in Virginia. We are learning how many great rivers help to make up the Ohio, and what an important region the Ohio valley was to the young country east of the mountains.

The settlements of which we have just read were all south of the Ohio river, for north of the river the Americans did not possess the land. This means that the country which now makes up the states of Ohio, Indiana, and Illinois was in foreign hands. The people were largely French and Indians, but they were governed by the British.

In order to defeat the Americans, the British, in all the years of the Revolutionary War, were stirring up the Indian tribes against the patriots. Just as St. Leger had Indian allies in New York, so British agents bribed the Indians of the West and South to fight and make as much trouble as possible.

George Rogers Clark was a young Virginian who had gone out to Kentucky, which then belonged to the mother state. He heard that Colonel Henry Hamilton, who commanded the British at Detroit, was persuading the Indians of that region to attack the frontier. He set out for Virginia, saw Patrick Henry, the governor, Thomas Jefferson, and other leading men, and gained permission to gather an army. This was in 1777, the year of Oriskany and Saratoga. He spent the winter enlisting soldiers, gathering his forces at Pittsburg.

FRONTIER SOLDIERS AND STATESMEN 157

Late the next spring they went in boats down the Ohio to the point where the muddy waters of the Mississippi

Fig. 60. George Rogers Clark

come in from the north. This alone was a journey of a thousand miles.

Up the Mississippi from that place was Kaskaskia, on the Illinois side. It is now a very small village, but it is the oldest town on the Mississippi river and was the first capital of Illinois. In the time of the Revolution it was governed by the British, although most of the people were French. Clark and his little army soon seized the place and made the people promise obedience to the new government.

There was another important old place called Vincennes, on the Wabash river, in what is now Indiana.

When Colonel Hamilton heard what Clark was doing he led an army of five hundred men, many of whom were Indians, from Detroit to Vincennes. It took them more than two months to make the journey. Clark sent some of his men with boats and provisions and cannon down the Mississippi, up the Ohio, and up the Wabash. He, with most of his little force, went across the prairie. It was a winter march and they had to wade through flood waters for a part of the way.

He found the food and the guns and soon captured Hamilton and his army. This was the last of British government between the Ohio river and the Great Lakes. At the close of the war the American messengers, who were in Paris arranging for peace, could say that they already had possession of all the land this side of the Mississippi, so no excuse was left for the British to claim it. In this way one frontier soldier saved several great states for his country.

The frontiersmen had beaten Cornstalk at Point Pleasant in 1774. Clark had won the prairie country five years later; and the next year, 1780, saw the great victory of Kings Mountain.

Lord Cornwallis was now chief general of the British. He had conquered the southern colonies, the Carolinas

FRONTIER SOLDIERS AND STATESMEN 159

and Georgia. Two of his officers, Tarleton and Ferguson, were brave and active commanders, and they were running over the country east of the mountains keeping the patriots down. Ferguson gathered together many American Tories and drilled them to march and fight.

The Watauga men, just over the mountains to the west, were loyal patriots. Ferguson heard of them and

FIG. 61. ON THE FRENCH BROAD, BETWEEN ASHEVILLE AND KNOXVILLE

sent them a stormy message. He told them to keep still or he would come over and scatter them and hang their leading men.

They were not used to talk of this kind and they determined to teach Ferguson a lesson. Isaac Shelby rode in hot haste from his home to John Sevier's log house on the Nolichucky river. When he arrived he found all the neighbors there; for Sevier had made a barbecue, and there was to be a big horse race, with running and wrestling matches. Shelby took Sevier off by himself and told him about Ferguson. They agreed to call together the mountain men and go over the Great Smokies to punish the British general.

On September 25, 1780, they came together at Sycamore Shoals on the Watauga river. Almost everybody was there, women and children as well as men. Four hundred sturdy men came from Virginia under William and Arthur Campbell. These two leaders and most of the men in the valley were sons of old Scotch Covenanters, and they were determined to win. A stern Presbyterian minister, the Reverend Samuel Doak, was there. He had as much fight in him as any of them, and as they stood in their rough hunter's garb he called upon God for help, preaching to them from the words, "The sword of the Lord and of Gideon."

They set out at once through the mountains, driving beef cattle for part of their food supply, and every man armed with rifle, tomahawk, and scalping knife. Roosevelt says there was not a bayonet or a tent in their army. The trail was stony and steep, and in the higher mountains they found snow. They marched as quickly as they could, for they wanted to catch Ferguson before Cornwallis could send more soldiers to help him.

On the way several hundred men from North Carolina, under Benjamin Cleveland, joined them. They had appointed no commander when they started, but on the march they chose one of the Campbells from Virginia.

When Ferguson found that they were pursuing him and that he must fight, he took up a strong position on Kings Mountain, in the northwest corner of South

Carolina. This hill was well chosen, for it stood by itself and on one side was too steep for a force to climb.

Ferguson called his foes a "swarm of backwoodsmen," but he knew that they could fight, or he would not have posted his own army with so much care. He felt sure of success, however, and thought that Heaven itself could hardly drive him off that hill.

As the patriot leaders drew near the British camp they saw that many of their men were too weary to overtake the swift and wary Ferguson, should he try to get away. So they picked out about half of the force, nearly a thousand mounted men. These men rode all night, and the next day approached the hill. Those who had lost their horses on the way hurried on afoot and arrived in time to fight. When close at hand the riders tied their horses in the woods, and the little army advanced to the attack on foot.

They moved up the three sides of the hill. Ferguson was famous for his bayonet charges, and the patriots had no bayonets. So when the British rushed down on the center of the advancing line the mountaineers gave way and the enemy pursued them down the hill. Then the backwoodsmen on the flanks rushed in and poured shot into the backs of the British. Turning to meet these new foes, the regulars were again chased up the hill and shot by the men who had fled from their bayonets. Thus shrewd tactics took the place of weapons. At length the gallant Ferguson was killed, the white flag was hoisted, and the firing stopped. Many British were slain, and all the rest, save a very few who escaped in the confusion, were made prisoners.

It was a wonderful victory for the men from the valley. They had come from a region of which Cornwallis had hardly dreamed, and they had destroyed one of his armies and killed one of his best commanders. The battle turned the tide of the Revolution in the South, but the

FIG. 62. JOHN SEVIER

victors hurried back as quickly as they had come. They were not fitted for a long campaign, and, besides, they had left their homes dangerously open to attacks from savages. It was, however, the one battle of the Revolution against white foes alone that was planned, fought, and won by the men of the frontier.

As soon as John Sevier returned to the valley he found plenty of Indian fighting to do. He was skilled in this, and with the Watauga men, who called him "Chucky Jack" and were devoted to him, he was a terror to the red men of the southern mountains. He knew all their tricks and how to give them back what he called "Indian play." At one time he took a band of his followers and made a daring ride into the wildest of the Great Smokies, to attack some hostile tribes. He burned their villages, destroyed their corn, killed and captured some of their warriors, and got away before they could gather their greater numbers to crush him.

We must not forget James Robertson, who all this time was doing his part of the farming and the fighting and the planning for the new settlements. Already the Watauga country began to have too many people and was too thickly settled to suit his temper, and he was thinking much about the wilderness beyond, near the lower part of the Cumberland river. In a great bend on the south bank of that stream he founded Nashborough in 1779, naming it in honor of Oliver Nash, governor of North Carolina. Five years later it became Nashville, and now we do not need to explain where it was.

Robertson went out by the Cumberland Gap, but soon left Boone's road and went toward the west, following the trails. When he and his followers reached the place and decided upon it as suitable for settlement, they planted a field of corn, to have something to depend on for food later.

The next autumn a large party of settlers went out to Nashborough. Robertson's family went with them. They did not go through the woods, but took boats to go down the Tennessee river. Their course led them along the Tennessee to the Ohio, then up the Ohio a few miles to the mouth of the Cumberland, and up the Cumberland to their new home. They had a long, dangerous voyage, and some of the party were killed, for the savages fired on them from the banks.

One of the boats, carrying twenty-eight grown people and children, had a number of cases of smallpox on board. The Indians attacked this boat and killed or captured the four sick travelers. For their deed the savages were badly punished, for they took the disease, which soon spread widely among the tribes.

FIG. 63. JAMES ROBERTSON

For a long time after Nashville was begun the pioneers had fierce encounters with the Indians, and in spite of all their care many lives were lost. Robertson was the strong man of the place, and was rewarded with the confidence of the people.

When Tennessee became a state he helped to make its constitution. He was a member of the state Senate in 1798, and lived long enough to keep some of the Indians from helping the British in the War of 1812. He died in 1814.

He was brave, and willing to endure hardship, discomfort, and suffering in a good cause. He went alone over the snows to Kentucky to get powder, and returned

FRONTIER SOLDIERS AND STATESMEN 165

in time to save the little town from destruction. The Indians killed his own son, but he would not give up the settlement. Plain man though he was, he gained honor from the men of his time, and wrote his name on the pages of American history.

We must learn a little more of Isaac Shelby, whom we have seen fighting hard at Point Pleasant and Kings Mountain. He was born in the Great Valley, at Hagerstown. When he was twenty-one years old he moved to Tennessee and then across to Kentucky. He fought in the Revolution in other battles besides that of Kings Mountain, and before he went to Kentucky he had helped to make laws in the legislature of North Carolina.

FIG. 64. SEVIER MONUMENT, KNOXVILLE

It is rather strange to read that Kentucky was made a "county" of Virginia. This was in 1776. In 1792, largely through Shelby's efforts, Kentucky was separated from Virginia and became a state by itself. It was the first state beyond the mountains, being four years older than Tennessee and eleven years ahead of Ohio.

Isaac Shelby was the first governor of Kentucky, from 1792 to 1796, and years later he was governor again. He fought in the War of 1812, and his name is preserved in Shelbyville, a town of Kentucky. The Blue Grass region has been called the "dark and bloody ground" from the strifes of the red tribes and the troublous days of the first settlers, but Shelby lived to see it the center of a prosperous state.

John Sevier, too, had more honors than those of a noble soldier. In front of the courthouse at Knoxville is a plain stone monument raised in his memory (Fig. 64), and down a side street is an old dwelling, said to be an early statehouse of the commonwealth which is still associated with his name. In 1785 the state of "Franklin" was organized and named in honor of the illustrious Benjamin; but North Carolina, being heartily opposed to the whole proceeding, put an end to it without delay. Sevier, as governor of the would-be state, was imprisoned, but escaped, to the delight of his own people, who were always loyal to him. They sent him to Congress in a few years and in 1796 made him the first governor of Tennessee. He enjoyed many honors until his death in 1815, which came soon after that of his more quiet friend, James Robertson. Both of these wilderness men had much to do with planting the American flag between the Appalachian mountains and the Mississippi river.

FIG. 65. OLD STATEHOUSE AT KNOXVILLE

CHAPTER XIV

CITIES OF THE SOUTHERN MOUNTAINS

In the old days it took the traveler weeks to go from Pennsylvania or the Potomac river to the valley of east Tennessee. He might camp in the woods, living on the few provisions he could carry and on what he could shoot in the forest, or he might share the humble homes of chance settlers on the way.

Now he enters a vestibuled train and is rolled over a smooth iron road along the streams and between the mountains. Starting one day, he will find when he wakes the next morning that the sun is rising over the Great Smokies, while around him are the rich rolling fields that border the Tennessee river.

If the traveler wishes to see the land and learn what men have done in a hundred years, he will leave the train at Knoxville. A carriage or an electric car will carry him between blocks of fine buildings to a modern hotel, where he will find food and bed and places to read, write, rest, or do business, as he likes. Around him is a busy city stretching up and down its many hills. Before long he will wander down to the banks of the Tennessee river and see the boats tied at the wharf, or he will cross the great bridge to the hills beyond and look back over the city.

On those hilltops are pits dug in the woods, and some veteran of the Union or the Confederate army will tell him that these are ammunition pits. The old soldier will point across to where Fort Sanders stood, and will

Fig. 66. Street in Knoxville

describe those days in 1863 when Longstreet came up and laid siege to the town, which was garrisoned by Burnside and his army.

Our traveler need do little more than cross the great bridge at Knoxville to find quarries of marble; and if he

CITIES OF THE SOUTHERN MOUNTAINS 169

goes up and down for a few miles, he will see rich deposits of this stone. It is prized because it shows many colors, — cream, yellow, brown, red, pink, and blue. The colors often run into each other in curious and fantastic ways, and the slabs and blocks when polished are beautiful indeed. These marbles have been used to adorn

FIG. 67. ON THE CAMPUS OF THE UNIVERSITY OF TENNESSEE

some of the finest buildings in America, including the National Capitol.

Around Knoxville are fine farms also, just as we find them about Harrisburg, Hagerstown, Winchester, and almost everywhere else in the Great Valley. Our view (Fig. 52) is taken near Knoxville and shows sloping fields always ready to bear good crops. The soils have been made by the wasting of the top parts of these same beds of marble and of other rocks found along with it.

In Knoxville, on the edge of the city, is the University of Tennessee, with many buildings upon its campus. It is an excellent school and an old one as well, having been founded in 1794. It was first named Blount College, from one of the prominent public men of the valley at that time, and is now one of the foremost schools of the South.

Only seven years before that date two old Revolutionary soldiers rode through the woods and picked out these lands, which were given to them as a reward for their service in the war. Here they built as a defense against the savages a wooden fort, with log cabins at the corners and a stockade with a stout barred gate. Such a fort was greatly needed in those days whenever a new settlement was made. After the two soldiers had planted corn they went back to North Carolina to bring their families over the mountains. This was the beginning of Knoxville, which grew up around the fort and soon spread over the hills and down to the river. The settlement was named in honor of Henry Knox, who was an able general in the Revolution and a good friend of George Washington.

Now the railroads reach out in every direction. They bring in the iron ore and the limestones of the valley. They also run up into the Cumberland Gap, and to Harriman, Tennessee, and bring back stores of coal, thus making Knoxville a place for working iron. To the east the Southern Railroad leads up the French Broad (Fig. 61) through deep gorges into the heart of the Great Smokies at Asheville, and across the Blue Ridge to the lowlands of North Carolina.

CITIES OF THE SOUTHERN MOUNTAINS 171

All this is very different from the samp mortars and the puncheon floors of early times, but the pioneers had a keen eye for the soil and the waters and the trees, and it is these which have helped to make the valley rich to-day.

We must not forget that off to the west James Robertson had founded a city that is even older than

Fig. 68. Marble Quarry near Knoxville

Knoxville. In the great bend of the Cumberland, on its south bank, in northern Tennessee, stands Nashville, as we have already seen.

If we visit a large city in one of the countries of Europe, we are quite likely to be told, or to read in our guidebook, that its history goes back hundreds of years, and any town that was started only a hundred years ago would there seem young. But we measure age differently in America, and a town like Nashville, founded in 1780, we think is old indeed. It is not easy to remember, as we ride along the streets and see the shops and mansions of Nashville to-day, that this was once a place of log cabins, and that the first settlers had to sleep always with one ear open for the Indian's war cry.

That James Robertson had to learn to read from his wife did not keep Nashville from becoming one of the centers of education and refinement in the South. It would take several lines to record the names of all the colleges and universities that now have their seat in this city. Robertson was the sort of man who, with the opportunities of to-day, might have been the president of one of these schools, or he might perhaps have gained a fortune with which to help in their support. Farther west, on the Mississippi river, stands Memphis, a city still larger than Nashville; indeed, few southern states can boast of so many cities as Tennessee possesses. Besides these, there are fertile valleys, fine rivers and mountains, productive forests, beds of iron ore and coal, comfortable farms, and thriving towns. The state is rich, too, in historical associations. Every part of Tennessee saw the dark days of the Civil War, and in the fields south of Nashville a great battle was fought.

When John Sevier went down the Tennessee river on his Indian raids he noticed that the stream, making a great bend, turns away from the valley and flows by a deep gorge through the highlands of the Cumberland plateau. We can take the train now at Knoxville, and a

CITIES OF THE SOUTHERN MOUNTAINS 173

ride of a little more than a hundred miles will bring us to this place.

By the river is a steep, high ground known as Cameron hill. Let us go up to the top and look around. Stretching away at our feet on the east is Chattanooga. Part of the city as we see it from Cameron hill is shown in the picture (Fig. 70). Beyond is the Tennessee, and we

FIG. 69. STATE HOUSE, NASHVILLE

are looking up the river to the northeast. The bridge which we see is the only bridge across the river at Chattanooga, even though it is now a large and busy city. In the distance is high ground, a part of Missionary Ridge, famous in the story of the Civil War.

If we turn around and look southward, we shall see Lookout Mountain, rising fifteen hundred feet above the river. A battle was fought on the steep slopes of this mountain also; and a few miles to the southeast is Chickamauga, one of the bloodiest battle grounds of the war. On the edge of the city, kept with care, is the National Cemetery, where rest the bodies of more than twelve thousand soldiers, northern and southern, who perished in the neighborhood of Chattanooga. Now all the region is peaceful, and only the tablets of iron and bronze, set up by the government on every battlefield in the neighborhood, tell the story of the conflict as it raged about the city.

Like Knoxville, Chattanooga has much coal and iron, is the center of a number of railways, and does much business. The railways run up the valley to Virginia, and south to Atlanta and elsewhere in Georgia. They stretch even further southward to Mobile and New Orleans, while the lines to the west reach Memphis and Nashville. Chattanooga is sometimes called the "Gate City" because it stands near the opening of the Great Valley into the wide plains along the gulf of Mexico. The place, originally called Ross's Landing, was not settled until 1836, when Knoxville and Nashville were about fifty years old. It has a noble site and may well become a great city.

Here passed the boats that bore the first settlers to Robertson's colony on the Cumberland. There are no Indians now to shoot from the banks, and you will see on the river only rafts of logs floating down from the forests in the mountains.

Atlanta also is often called the "Gate City" of the South. It stands more than a thousand feet above the sea, in northern Georgia, where the Appalachian mountain

FIG. 70. CHATTANOOGA, LOOKING NORTHEAST FROM CAMERON HILL. MISSIONARY RIDGE IN THE DISTANCE

range is tapering down toward the southern plains. Because Atlanta is so high it is cooler in summer than most southern cities, and is always free from the scourge of yellow fever and cholera.

It is a natural site for a city, for here at the end of the great mountain system the long lines of railway that follow the Atlantic coast swing around to the west, passing on to the Mississippi and down to Mobile and the ports on the gulf of Mexico. Other railways reach Atlanta from Chattanooga and Knoxville in the Great Valley, and still others lead the way to Savannah and the Atlantic coast. Thus twelve lines of railway reach out from Atlanta like the spokes of a wheel and connect the city with all parts of the South. Let us take a map of the United States and draw a line through Richmond, Louisville, Nashville, and New Orleans. Notice how many states lie southeast of this line, and remember that of all the towns which they contain Atlanta is the largest and most important. Indeed, in trade and influence it surpasses many northern cities which are much larger.

Atlanta saw stirring times in the Civil War. It was small then, having but about ten thousand people. In 1864 most of it was burned to the ground, and we may truly say that it has grown to its present size in the short period since that time. To-day its population numbers more than one hundred thousand. During the recent Spanish War the Department of the Gulf made its headquarters here, so that Atlanta appears to be sought both in war and in peace. The city was used as the capital of Georgia soon after the Civil War, and in 1877

Fig. 71. Atlanta: Broad Street, looking North

the people of the state voted that it should always be the seat of government. Since that time they have erected a capitol costing a million dollars, adorning the interior with marbles from their own quarries.

A few years ago an exposition was held at Atlanta to show the world the achievements and hopes of the great South. Everybody knew that the South raised cotton, but Atlanta wished to prove that the South could also

FIG. 72. FULTON BAG AND COTTON MILLS, ATLANTA

spin and weave her famous product. Mr. W. G. Atkinson was the governor of Georgia at that time. During the exposition a day was chosen in which something unusual should be done. Men went out into a field in the morning and picked some cotton. It was ginned and spun and woven in double-quick time. Then tailors took some of the cloth, cut it, fitted it, and sewed it into a suit of clothes. Governor Atkinson put on the suit and visited the grounds of the exposition. In the morning the cotton was in the field, in the evening

CITIES OF THE SOUTHERN MOUNTAINS 179

it was on the governor. Suits are not made so quickly as that on ordinary days, but the South spins and weaves millions of dollars' worth of cotton, turning the mill wheels with southern coal or with the waters of swift southern streams.

Atlanta is not only at the southern end of the mountains, but it is on the divide which separates the streams of the gulf from those of the Atlantic. On the one hand, not far away, is the Ocmulgee, flowing to the ocean, while westward, and distant but a few miles, the Chattahoochee flows toward the gulf. The latter river has been harnessed by man, and eleven thousand horse power measures the amount of energy that can be carried over the wires to Atlanta to move its cars and turn the wheels of its factories.

FIG. 73. GEORGIA INSTITUTE OF TECHNOLOGY, ATLANTA

The mills not only spin the cotton of the gulf plains but also turn out fertilizers, work up the timber of the region, and make a multitude of other things to swell the city's trade with her neighbors.

Appropriate to her needs, Atlanta has had since 1887 a school of technology, in which she teaches her sons

FIG. 74. IRON FURNACE, BIRMINGHAM

how to develop the great resources of the South. Here are shops and departments of engineering, and, not least, instruction in making textiles, so that the cotton of southern fields need no longer go to Massachusetts or to England to be spun and woven.

The youngest great town of the southern mountain region was started on an old cotton plantation in 1871, thirty-four years before the writing of these lines. The people knew that in Alabama as well as in Tennessee coal and iron are found close together. So men built an iron town and called it, after one of the greatest furnace towns in the world, Birmingham. It is a noisy, busy place, with wide streets, swift electric cars, and blazing furnaces. To see it grow is like watching a new Pittsburg rise up in the heart of the South.

From the Berkshire country at the north to the southern end of the Appalachians, there are to-day thriving towns and fertile fields. No longer does the mountain wall cut off the products of the West from the markets of the East. Yet hardly a hundred years ago the eastern strip of country was practically shut off from the whole territory drained by the Ohio and Mississippi rivers. Indian trails and rough roads were the only means of communication between the two sections. Great as are the natural resources of both regions, their prosperity has been bound up in the development of roads and railways, and is due in large measure to the energy, foresight, and self-sacrifice of those who crossed the barrier and made it easy for others to follow them.

INDEX

Adams, Charles Francis, cited, 7
Adams, John Quincy, 100
Adirondacks, 32
Albany, N.Y., 6, 10, 15, 16
Alexander, Mt., 130
Alexandria, Va., 41, 86
Allegheny Front, 74, 78, 80, 82
Allegheny Portage Railway, 75, 76, 80
Allegheny river, 111
Allentown, Pa., 79
Altoona, Pa., 77; description of, 81
Amsterdam, N.Y., 20
Ann, Fort, 32
Annapolis, Md., 88
Antietam, 132
Appalachians, southern, 174
"Arks" on the Susquehanna, 41
Arnold, Benedict, 37
Atkinson, Gov. W. G., 178
Atlanta, Ga., 174–180
Auburn, N.Y., 57

Bald Eagle valley, 80
Baltimore, Md., 53, 86, 101; growth of, 107
Baltimore and Ohio Railroad, 99, 101, 102, 110
Barges on the Ohio, 116, 118
Barton, Clara, cited, 82
Bay Road, Mass., 4
Bedford, Pa., 71, 77
Bemis Heights, 38
Bennington, Vt., 38
Berkshires, 5; railway through, 9, 10
Bethlehem, Pa., 79
Binghamton, N.Y., 52
Birmingham, Ala., 181
Black Rock (Buffalo), 47

"Blackbeard," 130
Blockhouse at Pittsburg, 112
Blount College, 170
Blue Grass country, 127, 151, 166
Blue mountain, 79
Blue Ridge mountains, 88, 130
Boone, Daniel, early life, 144; training, 145; portrait, 145; moves to North Carolina, 146; serves with Braddock, 146; camps in Kentucky, 147; visits Cumberland Gap, 148; founds Boonesborough 148; buys lands of the Indians, 149; marks out the Wilderness road, 149
Boonesborough, 148
Boston, Mass., 1, 2, 7, 12
Braddock, General, 69, 90, 91, 146
Braddock, Pa., 83
Brant, Joseph, 33
Bristol, Tenn., 134
British, in New York, 32; in the Ohio country, 156
Brownsville, Pa., 93, 117
Buffalo, 52, 57, 60, 110; growth of, 61
Burgoyne, General, 32, 37
Burnside, General, 168
Business, increase of, 114, 118

Cambria Steel Company, 83
Cameron hill, 173
Campbell, William and Arthur, 160
Canajoharie, N.Y., 24
Canals, 44; Erie, 7, 46, 48, 50–52; Pennsylvania, 74; Chesapeake and Ohio, 98–101, 107; Delaware and Hudson, 53; at Louisville, Ky., 127
Carlisle, Pa., 71, 79, 132
Carroll, Charles, 101

Carry to Schenectady, the, 19, 22
Catch-me-if-you-can, 2
Catskill mountains, 15, 32
Chambersburg, Pa., 71, 132
Champlain, lake, 31, 37
Charlottesville, Va., 142
Chattahoochee river, 179
Chattanooga, Tenn., 135; description of, 173-175
Cherokee Indians, 139, 149
Chesapeake bay, 86
Chesapeake and Ohio canal, 107; building of, 98-101
Chicago, 110
Chickamauga, 174
Chissel, Fort, 135
Cincinnati, Ohio, description of, 123-127
Clark, George Rogers, raises an army, 156; portrait, 157; captures Kaskaskia and Vincennes, 158
Clay, Henry, stories of, 96, 114
Cleveland, Benjamin, 160
Clinch river, 134
Clinton, De Witt, 44, 49; stirs up legislature, 40; portrait, 43; train, 53, 54
Coal, 104, 118, 122, 153, 170, 181
Cohoes, N.Y., 22
Coke ovens, 108
Columbia, The, 2
Columbia, Pa., 69, 74, 76
Columbus, Ohio, 94
Conemaugh river, 75, 82
Conestoga creek, 67
Conestoga Traction Company, 70
Conestoga wagons, 77
Connecticut river, 4
Construction, early railway, 105
Cooper, Peter, 106
Cornstalk, 155
Cornwallis, Lord, 158
Cotton, 178
Cumberland, Fort, 89, 90; city of, 93, 95, 102
Cumberland Gap, 142, 148, 150, 152
Cumberland mountains, 134, 142
Cumberland river, 164, 174

Cumberland road, 93
Cunard, Samuel, 2
Cunard line, 2, 8

Dams, use of, 119
Danforth, Mr., and salt making, 27
Deerfield valley, 8
Delaware and Hudson Canal Company, 53
Delaware, Lackawanna and Western Railroad, 60
De-o-wain-sta, 23
Detroit, 41, 156
Dickens, Charles, 126
Dinwiddie, Governor, 89
Doak, Rev. Samuel, 160
Dongan, Gov. Thomas, 40
Dunlap's creek, 96
Dunmore, Lord, 155
Duquesne, Fort, 91
Dutch, in New-York, 14, 18, 31

Earle, Mrs. Alice Morse, cited, 55
Easton, Pa., 79
Edward, Fort, 31
Emerson, Ralph Waldo, cited, 1
Empire State Express, 56
England, interest of, in fur trade, 18; railways of, 55
Erie canal, 7, 42, 46, 48, 50-52
Erie, lake, 18, 42, 98
Erie Railroad, 60
Euphrates river, 130

Fairfax, Lord William, 88
Falls of the Ohio, 127, 146, 152
Farms in Pennsylvania, 66
"Feeders" of Erie canal, 52
Ferguson, Patrick, 159
Finley, John, 146, 148
Fishing interests, 104
Flag, perhaps the first American, 34
Flatboats, 117
Floyd, Gen. William, 22
Forbes's road, 71
Forts: Orange, 17; Stanwix, 22, 23, 34, 37, 61, 149; Schuyler, 23; Johnson, 26; Edward, 31; Ann, 32; Ticonderoga, 32, 37, 38;

INDEX

Cumberland, 89, 90; Duquesne, 91; Chissel, 135; Sanders, 168
Franklin, Benjamin, 4, 69, 130
"Franklin," state of, 166
Frederick, Md., 93
French, in Ohio country, 89
French and Indian War, 69
French Broad river, 135, 159, 170
Frostburg, Md., 90, 93
Fur trade, 18, 24, 40
Furnaces near Pittsburg, 121

Gansevoort, Col. Peter, 34.
Gas, natural, 120
"Gate City," the, 174
Genesee road, 24, 25
Genesee street, Utica, 23
Geneva, 24, 25
George, Mt., 130
Georgetown, D.C., 100
Georgia Institute of Technology, 179
Germans in Pennsylvania, 66; in Tennessee, 136
Ginseng, 24
Gist, Christopher, 89
Glass mills, 122
Gray, Captain, 2
Great Kanawha river, 155
Great Smoky mountains, 134, 170
Great Valley, the, 71, 130, 132, 134, 136, 139.
Gulliver's Travels, 150
Gypsum, 104

Hagerstown, Md., 25, 132, 165
Half Moon, the, 15
Halifax, 2
Hambright's Hotel, 70
Hamburg-American line, 108
Hamilton, Col. Henry, 156
Hancock, Gov. John, 2
Hanks, Abraham, 149
Harlem, 14
Harpers Ferry, 107, 130, 132
Harriman, Tenn., 170
Harrisburg, Pa., 74, 85, 132; description of, 78
Henry, Patrick, 156
Herkimer, Nicholas, 29, 33, 35, 36

Hessians, 33, 38
Hill, Gen. A. P., 142
Hit or Miss, the, 77
Hiwassee river, 135
Hollidaysburg, Pa., 74
Holston river, 134
Honesdale, Pa., 53
Hoosac mountain, 5, 8
Hoosac tunnel, 9–11
Hoosick river, 5
Housatonic river, 5
Howe, General, 32
Hudson, Henry, 15, 16
Hudson river, 15
Huguenots, 136
Hulbert, cited, 105

Illinois, 158
Indiana, 158
Indians, 144, 149, 163, 164; in New York, 14, 17, 18, 33; at Watauga, 138; at Point Pleasant, 155
Indies, hope of reaching, 15
Iron works, 121, 129, 170, 180
Iroquois Indians, 18

Jackson, "Stonewall," 133
James river, 133; gap, 134
Jefferson, Thomas, 156
Johns Hopkins University, 108
Johnson, Fort, 26
Johnson, John, 36
Johnson, Sir William, 20
Johnstown, N.Y., 20
Johnstown, Pa., 75, 76, 82
Joppa, 92
Juniata river, 74

Kaskaskia, Ill., 116, 157
Kentucky, 127, 154, 164; becomes a state, 165
Kings Mountain, 158, 160
Knights, Sarah, 4
Knox, Gen. Henry, 170
Knoxville, 134, 166, 170

Lake Shore Railroad, 110
Lancaster, Pa., 65, 72, 78
Lancaster pike, 65, 67, 70

Lee, Arthur, 113
Lee, Richard Henry, 98
Lee, Gen. Robert E., 132
Legislators allowed boat hire, 87
Lewis, Andrew, 155
Licking river, 124
Limestones, 104, 132, 151, 169
Lincoln, Abraham, 117, 149
Little Falls, N.Y., 22, 42
Little Tennessee river, 135
Liverpool, 110
Locks, 45
Logan, 155
London, 110
Long House, the, 18
Longstreet, General, 168
Lookout Mountain, 173
Losantiville, 124
Louisville, 117, 127
Lulbegrud creek, 151
Luray, 131, 132
Lyell, Sir Charles, cited, 126

McClellan, General, 132
Mail, first, received at Utica, 24
Mail bags, race of the, 109
Mail coaches, 94
Manhattan island, 14, 15
Marble, 104, 168, 171
Maryland, 86
Memphis, 172
Middlesboro, 153
Milestone on Braddock's road, 90
Missionary Ridge, 173
Mobile, 174
Mohawk valley, 16-19, 31, 42, 59
Monongahela river, 93, 96, 111
Morris, Gouverneur, 42
Mount Vernon, 41, 86

Nash, Oliver, 163
Nashborough (Nashville), 163, 171, 173
National Road, the, 91, 93, 96, 123
New Amsterdam, 14
New Jersey, Scotch-Irish in, 66
New Netherlands, 14
New river (Great Kanawha), 134

New York Central Railway, 20, 30, 58, 60, 62
New York City, 2, 7, 14
New York state, 27; well adapted for canal, 44
Newburg, N.Y., 60
Noah's Ark, 49
Nolichucky river, 159
Norfolk and Western Railway, 133
North Adams, Mass., 5
North American Review, 102
North Carolina, 137, 146
North-German Lloyd line, 108

Ocmulgee river, 179
Ogden, Utah, 109
Ohio Company, 88
Ohio country, French in, 89
Ohio river, 76, 98, 111, 123, 127, 152
Oil City, 120
Omaha, 109
Oneida Indians, 17
Oneida Carrying Place, 22
Onondaga salt, 27, 113
Ontario, lake, 18, 22, 33
Oriskany, 29, 30, 35
Oswego, 32
Oswego river, 22
Otsego lake, 98
Oyster industry, 104

"Packers," 72
Packets, 50
Parton, James, cited, 120
Penn, William, 66
Pennsylvania, settlement of, 66
Pennsylvania Railroad, 77-85
"Pennsylvania Dutch," 66
Pennsylvania canal, 74
Phelps, Abner, 9
Philadelphia, 41, 63
Pike, Pittsburg, 72; Frederick, 93
Pineville gap, 143, 147
Pittsburg, 64, 71, 75, 83, 107, 156; description of, 111, 115, 120, 122; pike, 72
Pittsfield, Mass., 5
Point Pleasant, 155

INDEX

Portage Railway, Allegheny, 75, 76, 80
Post, John, 23, 24
Potomac Company, 99
Potomac river, 86, 106
Powell, Ambrose, 142
Powell's river, 134, 142
Prairies in Kentucky, 152
Princeton College, 66
Providence, R.I., 4
Puncheon floors, 140

Queen City, the, 124
Queenstown, 110
Quincy, Mass., 53

Railways: through the Berkshires, 9, 10; from Albany to Schenectady, 9, 53; early, 53, 56; opposition to, 55; growth of, 60, 109, 181; West Shore, 59; Erie, 60; New York Central, 20, 30, 58, 60, 62; Wabash, 102; Baltimore and Ohio, 99, 101, 102, 110; Southern Pacific, 109; Union Pacific, 109; Lake Shore, 110; Norfolk and Western, 133; Southern, 134, 170
Reading, Pa., 79
Red Star line, 108
Redstone, 117
Richardson, Judge John, 46
Rivers important in a country's growth, 5–7, 16, 17, 24, 26, 31, 41, 122, 126, 133
Roads, in New England, 4, 6, 7; stage, 64; development of, 72; indifference to, 87; national interest in, 92; Braddock's, 90; Cumberland, 93; Frederick, 93; National, 91, 93, 96; Wilderness (Boone's trail, Kentucky road, Virginia road, Caintuck Hog road), 127, 149
Roanoke, 134
Robertson, James, goes to Watauga, 137; pacifies the Indians, 139; helps protect the new settlement, 155; founds Nashborough, 163; trusted by the people, 164; portrait, 164; ability, 172
Rochester, N.Y., 25, 52
Rochester, Colonel, 26, 41, 61, 132
"Rolling roads," 88
Rome, 22, 46, 61
Roosevelt, Theodore, cited, 137, 140, 160
Ross's Landing, 174

Sails on cars, 105
St. Clair, General, 124
St. Leger, General, 33, 61
Salt, 27, 61, 113
Samp mortars, 21
San Francisco, 109
Saratoga, 38
Schenectady, 19, 42, 47, 61
"Schonowe," 19
Schuyler, Fort (Utica), 23
Schuyler, Han Yost, 37
Schuylerville, 38
Scotch-Irish, 66, 136
Seneca river, 24
Seneca lake, 25
Settlement: in New England, 4; in New York, 14, 24; in Pennsylvania, 66; in the Ohio country, 117; in Tennessee, 135, 170; in Kentucky, 148
Sevier, John, goes to Watauga, 138; fights on the frontier, 155; plans to attack Ferguson, 160; returns home, 162; portrait, 162; monument to, 165; other honors, 166; on the Tennessee river, 172
Shelby, Isaac, 155, 159, 165
Shelbyville, 165
Shenandoah valley, 88, 107, 130, 132
Sheridan, 133
Shippensburg, Pa., 71
Shreve, Captain, 117
Slate, 104
"Smoky City, The," 120
South Mountain, Pa., 132
Southern Pacific Railway, 22
Southern Railway, 134, 170
Speed of early trains, 105

Spotswood, Alexander, 129
Springfield, Mass., 6, 10
Stanwix, Fort, 22, 23, 34, 37, 61, 149
Stark, General, 38
Staunton, Va., 135
Steamboats, 118
Stephenson, George, 53
Stillwater, 38
Susquehanna valley, 26, 41, 46, 104
Swift Run Gap, 130
Sycamore Shoals, 160
Sydney, Australia, 109
Syracuse, 27, 52, 57, 61

Tarleton, Colonel, 159
Teamsters of early days, 64, 69
Tennessee, 134, 154, 164, 172; University of, 170
Tennessee river, 134, 142, 163, 167, 172, 174
Ticonderoga, 32, 37, 38
Tidewater country, 87, 130
Timber, 104, 180
Toll houses, 68, 87
Toll rates, 94
Tom Thumb, 106
Trails, old, 4, 6, 17, 19, 22, 25, 28, 72
Tramways in England, 54
Transylvania Company, 148
Travel, early, 5, 22, 56, 64, 91
Trow Plat, 23
Trunk line, 57
"Tubal Cain of Virginia," 129
Tudor, Frederick, 4
Twentieth Century Limited, 56

Union Pacific Railroad, 109
University of Tennessee, 170
Utica, 21, 23, 37, 57, 61

Valley of east Tennessee, 135; of Virginia, 132
Valley, the Great, 71, 130, 132, 134, 136, 139
Valleys as natural roads, 5–7, 16, 17, 22, 24, 26, 31, 41, 126, 133, 142, 152, 156
Van Curler, Arent, 17, 19, 57, 61
Vanderbilt, Cornelius, 58
Ventura, the, 109
Vincennes, Ind., 158
Virginia, 129, 154; valley of, 132

Wabash Railway Company, 102
Wabash river, 158
Walker, Dr. Thomas, 142
Ward, Nancy, 139
Washington, D.C., 91, 93, 94
Washington, George, 41, 60, 86, 112, 133; part taken by, in road making, 88–92, 98
Washington, Lawrence, 89
Watauga Settlement, 135–141, 144, 146, 159
Waterford, 47
West, the, 40, 60
Westfield valley, 6
West Shore Railway, 59
Wheeling, 94, 107, 122
White, Hugh, 21
Whitesboro, 21
Wilderness Road, 127, 149
Willett, Captain Marinus, 35
William and Mary College, 142
Wills creek, 89, 102
Wills mountain, 93
Winchester, Va., 132, 135
Windmills, Dutch, 15
Wood creek, 22, 42

Yadkin valley, North Carolina, 146